THE BOOK OF
MENTORS
HONORING
BOB PROCTOR

CREATED BY MULTI #1 INTERNATIONAL BEST-SELLING AUTHOR & AWARD WINNING SPEAKER ON HABITS

ERIK "MR AWESOME" SWANSON

HONORING BOB PROCTOR

THE BOOK OF MENTORS

Keys To Success Honoring Legacy
Legends Zig Ziglar, Bob Proctor,
Dr. Wayne Dyer, & Jim Rohn

HONORING
BOB PROCTOR

Orders by U.S. trade bookstores and wholesalers.

Email: *Team@IntegrityPub.com*

Manufactured and printed in the United States of America and distributed globally by Integrity Pub.

Library of Congress Control Number:
Hardback ISBN: 978-1-964330-02-0
Paperback ISBN: 978-1-964330-01-3

Celebrity Quotes

THE BOOK OF MENTORS

The Book of Mentors ~ Honoring Legacy Legends Zig Ziglar, Bob Proctor, Dr. Wayne Dyer, and Jim Rohn!

"Bravo, Bravo, Bravo! I want to compliment you in deciding to find a Mentor in your life. We all need them!"

Sir Bruno Serato ~ Philanthropist, Founder of Caterina's Club, CNN Man of the Year, Best-Selling Author, Owner and Chef of the Anaheim White House ~ www.AnaheimWhitehouse.com

"A true mentor can offer you invaluable insights and advice that will help you navigate challenges and opportunities throughout your life."

Brian Tracy ~ Author, Speaker, Motivator ~ www.BrianTracy.com

"I changed directions, but I never changed the dream!"

Rudy Ruettiger ~ Author, Speaker, Inspirational Mentor, The Real Rudy from the movie 'RUDY' ~ www.RudyRuettiger.com

"Mentorship is life! Increase your world by learning from those who have stepped into greatness before you, and then strive to become a Mentor to those who follow you in your footsteps in the future."

Erik "Mr. Awesome" Swanson ~ Author, Speaker, Habits Coach ~ www.SpeakerErikSwanson.com

"There are two ways to learn. One is from the books we read and the other is being around smarter people. We become the average of the people we spend most of our time with People who do not read are no better off than people who cannot read to quote Mark Twain."

Don Green ~ President of the Napoleon Hill Foundation, Author, Speaker, Mentor ~ www.NapHill.org

"Be curious about your available sources of mentorship. There is often much to learn from those we perceive as less experienced."

Paul Blanchard ~ Author, Speaker, Habits Coach ~ www.WholeBodyMindset.com

"Success isn't the Gold Medal. It's the Silver Medal. The Gold Medal is significance. You achieve significance by helping someone else succeed. That is true mentorship!"

Ruben Gonzalez ~ Author, Speaker, Four Time Olympian ~ www.TheLugeMan.com

"I have had some great mentors when I first started in the media business in NYC, that allowed me to take on some very tricky assignments at a very young age. Since then, I have been mentoring folks on a regular basis and it is incredibly satisfying to see them grow and succeed not only in business but also in their personal lives."

Larry Namer ~ Founder of E! Entertainment Television ~ www.EOnline.com

"Mentors are the teachers of life. 'If you give a man a fish, you feed him for a day. If you teach a man to fish, you feed him for a lifetime.' The mentors of life will perpetually become the heart and soul of progress and evolution in our world."

Jon Kovach Jr. ~ Author, Speaker, Mastermind Leader ~ www.SpeakerJonKovachJr.com

"Mentorship is a bridge between your VISION and its manifestation. It's having a Confidant by your side, who recognizes your greatness, and casts LIGHT on the path to accessing your Highest Self, and most elevated potential. Embracing the guidance of a mentor will INSPIRE and EMPOWER you to transform the ordinary into TRIUMPH. This sacred relationship evokes your BRILLIANCE, so you navigate through mists of uncertainty to the shores of CLARITY and ACHIEVEMENT."

Niurka ~ Transformation & Fulfillment Coach, NLP Master ~ www.NiurkaInc.com

"The gap between your divine potential and where you are today is called mentorship."

Darryll Stinson ~ Entrepreneur, Pastor, Speaker, Suicide Survivor ~ www.DarryllStinson.com

"A mentor is a great encourager. Mentorship is teaching from experience but deciding how to impart those lessons to others at the right times. Mentorship is all about experience that is shared with others. Then they encourage you to pursue the advice given."

Don Hobbs ~ Former President Success Magazine, Named Best Marketer by Tony Robbins, Co-Founder 7 Figure Coaching Secrets ~ www.DonHobbs.com

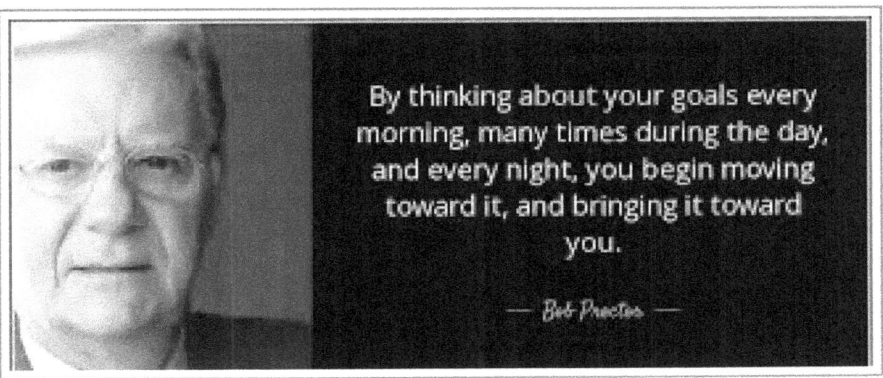

By thinking about your goals every morning, many times during the day, and every night, you begin moving toward it, and bringing it toward you.

— *Bob Proctor* —

Global Speakers Mastermind & Habitude Warrior Masterminds

Join us and become a member of our tribe! Our Global Speakers Mastermind is a virtual group of amazing thinkers and leaders who meet twice a month. Sessions are designed to be 'to the point' and focused while sharing fantastic techniques to grow your mindset as well as your pocketbooks. We also include famous guest speaker spots for our private Masterclasses. We also designate certain sessions for our members to mastermind with each other & and counsel on the topics discussed in our previous Masterclasses. It's time for you to join a tribe who truly cares about **YOU** and your future and start surrounding yourself with the famous leaders and mentors of our time. It is time for you to up-level your life, businesses, and relationships.

For more information to check out our Masterminds:
Team@HabitudeWarrior.com
www.DecideTobeAwesome.com

BECOME AN INTERNATIONAL
#1 BESTSELLING AUTHOR & SPEAKER

Habitude Warrior International has been highlighting award-winning Speakers and #1 Bestselling Authors for over 25 years. They know what it takes to become #1 in your field and how to get the best exposure around the world. If you have ever considered giving yourself the GIFT of becoming a well-known Speaker and a fantastically well known #1 Best-Selling Author, then you should email their team right away to find out more information in how you can become involved. They have the best of the best when it comes to resources in achieving the bestselling status in your particular field. Start surrounding yourself with the N.Y. Times Bestsellers of our time and start seeing your dreams become reality!

For more information to become a #1 Bestselling Author
& Speaker on our Habitude Warrior Conferences
Please text the word AUTHORS to 619-304-6268
And also go to:
www.DecideToBeAwesome.com

Acknowledgement to Bob Proctor

It is with immense respect and profound appreciation that I, along with the awesome team of authors in this series, extend our deepest gratitude to the esteemed Mr. Bob Proctor. His extraordinary commitment and contributions have profoundly influenced countless lives worldwide. Bob Proctor leaves behind a monumental legacy through his unparalleled mentorship and visionary leadership in the field of personal development.

We pay homage to his tireless dedication and exceptional training endeavors, including his groundbreaking teachings and motivational programs. His works, such as *You Were Born Rich* and numerous other transformative books and seminars, have reached far beyond the many who have drawn wisdom and inspiration from his teachings.

With the utmost sincerity, I express our collective thanks to Mr. Proctor, from the bottom of our hearts, for the myriad of connections and relationships he has enriched. His life's work continues to inspire us to forge stronger bonds, cultivate trust, and create genuine interactions with those we serve. May we all embody his teachings to elevate others and contribute to making this world an extraordinary place to live.

~ Erik "Mr. Awesome" Swanson ~ Multi #1 International Bestselling Author & Award-Winning Speaker

CONTENTS

Introduction

THE BOOK OF MENTORS

Welcome to *The Book of Mentors* book series — an extraordinary journey of transformation, guidance, and wisdom. In the pages that follow, you will find a riveting exploration of mentorship, leadership, and the indelible impact of some of the most legendary figures in the realm of personal and professional development. This series is a meticulously curated anthology that pays homage to Zig Ziglar, Bob Proctor, Dr. Wayne Dyer, and Jim Rohn—four individuals whose lives and teachings have left an indelible mark on the world.

Mentorship is a timeless concept, a sacred exchange of wisdom, and a guiding light that has illuminated the paths of countless individuals seeking direction, clarity, and purpose. In today's fast-paced and ever-evolving world, the need for authentic leaders and mentors has never been greater. *The Book of Mentors* series emerges as a crucial resource, a compass for those in pursuit of excellence, wisdom, and a life lived in alignment with their highest values.

The celebrity authors, accompanied by the founder and creator, Erik "Mr. Awesome" Swanson and the contributing co-authors in this distinguished series, are an elite assembly of thinkers, leaders, and change-makers. Together, they are creating an everlasting resource of wisdom, intertwining together the legacy of Legacy Legends with the contemporary insights and experiences of today's thought leaders. Their voice, stories, and wisdom are integral roles and lessons as we collectively honor the mentors who have paved the way for us all.

Volume One: Honoring Legacy Legend Zig Ziglar

Zig Ziglar was a master of motivation, a beacon of integrity, and a true champion of the human spirit. His teachings transcended the boundaries of sales and business, touching the hearts and minds of individuals from all walks of life. In the first volume of *The Book of Mentors*, we celebrate Zig's unparalleled ability to inspire action, ignite passion, and instill a deep-seated belief in the potential that resides within each of us. We delve into the core principles that defined Zig's legacy, exploring how his teachings continue to guide, motivate, and transform lives today.

Volume Two: Honoring Legacy Legend Bob Proctor

Bob Proctor was a luminary in the world of personal development, a sage who unraveled the mysteries of the human mind and unlocked the secrets to limitless potential. His teachings on the law of attraction, the power of thought, and the transformative potential of belief have left an indelible mark on the world. In this second volume, we pay tribute to Bob's profound wisdom, delving into the principles that fueled his teachings and exploring the ripple effects of his mentorship across the globe. You will discover a wealth of knowledge, inspiration, and transformation.

Volume Three: Honoring Legacy Legend Dr. Wayne Dyer

Dr. Wayne Dyer was a spiritual guide, a philosopher, and a beacon of light in the journey of self-discovery and spiritual awakening. His teachings on intention, the power of thought, and the connection between the spiritual and the material world have transformed the lives of millions. In this third volume, we honor Wayne's legacy, exploring the depth of his wisdom and the profound impact of his teachings on the world. Just like the *Gifts from Eykis*, here you'll find a sanctuary of wisdom, guiding readers on a journey of inner-exploration, self-realization, and transformative growth.

Volume Four: Honoring Legacy Legend Jim Rohn

Jim Rohn was a philosopher, a mentor, and a visionary in the world of personal development. His teachings on the art of living, the power of personal responsibility, and the importance of continuous learning have shaped the course of mentorship across the globe. In this final volume, we celebrate Jim's timeless wisdom, delving into the principles and practices that defined his teachings. We paint a portrait of a man whose legacy continues to inspire, educate, and elevate the lives of individuals around the world.

The Book of Mentors book series is more than just a collection of books —it is a movement, a legacy, and a testament to the transformative power of mentorship. We are creating a legacy resource that speaks to the heart of what it means to be a mentor, a leader, and a guide in this ever-changing world.

As you turn the pages of each volume, we invite you to immerse yourself in the teachings, the stories, and the wisdom that have shaped the lives of millions. This series is a call to action—a reminder that the journey of mentorship is a lifelong pursuit, a sacred exchange, and a path to transformation. Together, we honor the Legacy Legends, celebrate the mentors who have guided us, and pave the way for the next generation of leaders and changemakers.

The journey begins here, and the path ahead is rich with possibility.

Honoring Bob Proctor

A TRIBUTE TO A LEGACY LEGEND OF INSPIRATION & WISDOM

In the grand meaning of mentorship and transformative leadership, the leadership legacy created by Bob Proctor stands out with brilliance and strength. His life's work, a symphony of empowering words and uplifting teachings, finds a special place in the second volume of *The Book of Mentors ~ Honoring Legacy Legend Bob Proctor*, a unique endeavor created by Erik "Mr. Awesome" Swanson. Mr. Swanson is accompanied by 13 celebrity authors and 33 contributing co-authors. Bob Proctor is celebrated not just as a mentor among millions but as a beacon of wisdom and a paragon of positive influence.

Throughout the pages of this book, Proctor's legacy is personified in harmony with the stories and insights of authors who have themselves been touched by the magic of mentorship. They share, with reverence and authenticity, their journeys of trials and triumphs, all while standing on the shoulders of giants like Bob Proctor. It is a profound honor to pay tribute to a man whose messages and principles have shaped the course of mentorship across the globe. This book, and the voices within it, serve as a testament to the enduring power of Proctor's teachings, advocating for a world rich in guidance, support, and the transformative magic of mentorship.

The Book of Mentors series embarks on an unprecedented mission, honoring legacy legends like Zig Ziglar, Bob Proctor, Dr. Wayne Dyer, and Jim Rohn. This initiative is a beacon of innovation in the realm of mentorship, providing readers with a treasure trove of wisdom from those who have walked the path and learned from the best. As we delve into the pages of these dedicatory chapters and the book at large, we invite readers to explore, learn, and grow, drawing inspiration from Bob Proctor's life and the countless others who have been influenced by the power of mentorship. In doing so, we continue to weave the threads of mentorship through the fabric of society, ensuring that the legacy of Bob Proctor and other legends lives on for generations to come.

A Tribute to a Legacy Legend: Bob Proctor

Bob Proctor was more than just a motivational speaker or a self-help author; he was a visionary whose profound insights into the human psyche and the laws of the universe transformed countless lives across the globe. His unwavering dedication to unlocking human potential led him to explore the deepest philosophies of success and abundance, leaving a legacy rich with empowerment and enlightenment through works such as *You Were Born Rich*. In his influential role in the groundbreaking film *The Secret*, Proctor championed the belief that our thoughts create our reality, a powerful concept that has resonated with millions. As we embark on this tribute to his illustrious life and career, we celebrate a man whose teachings continue to inspire us to dream and to have the courage to achieve, profoundly altering the course of personal development history.

Bob Proctor was a towering figure in the landscape of personal development and self-help, whose teachings and writings have left an amazing mark around the world. Born into modest circumstances and initially lacking direction, Proctor's life underwent a profound transformation through his encounter with Napoleon Hill's *Think and Grow Rich*, a moment that catalyzed his lifelong commitment to exploring and teaching the principles of success and abundant living. His journey from a struggling individual to a respected guru in the self-help field exemplifies the principles he taught—principles that promise personal transformation through mental reconditioning and focused action.

Proctor's influence on personal development extended well beyond conventional self-help paradigms, touching on elements of spirituality, the power of positive thinking, and the laws of attraction. His approach was not merely theoretical but intensely practical, offering actionable guidance that resonated with people from all walks of life who sought clarity and success in their personal and professional endeavors. His work was grounded in the belief that individuals can change their circumstances and shape their reality through their thoughts and feelings.

Among his many contributions, Bob Proctor is best remembered for his book *You Were Born Rich* (1984), which outlines a framework for personal prosperity that anyone can follow. The book, rich with strategies and anecdotes, details how to unlock one's potential and harness the mental attitudes necessary for success. It emphasizes that wealth begins in the mind, and with the right mindset, one can attract riches in all areas of life.

Furthermore, Proctor's teachings gained additional fame through his involvement in the book and film *The Secret* (2006), where he discussed the law of attraction, which posits that like attracts like and that by emitting positive or negative thoughts, one can bring positive or negative experiences into one's life. This appearance helped propel the concept into global consciousness and underscored his role as a key proponent of this philosophy. *The Secret* brought these ideas to millions, making the law of attraction a household term and Proctor one of its most celebrated advocates.

Through these works and his numerous other writings and speeches, Bob Proctor carved a niche as a luminary in self-help, his teachings becoming a cornerstone for many in their personal and professional development. His ability to translate complex psychological and metaphysical concepts into accessible, actionable teachings has made him a beloved figure among those seeking to improve their lives. His legacy, therefore, is not just in the wealth of material he produced but in the profound impacts those materials had on the lives of his readers and listeners around the globe.

Early Life & Turning Point

Born on July 5, 1934, in Ontario, Canada, Bob Proctor grew up in an environment marked by ordinary expectations and modest means. His early years were not characterized by academic success or clear direction; in fact, his formal education concluded abruptly after a bandsaw accident at Danforth Tech, which left him with a wounded thumb and a wounded spirit, uncertain about his future—this period of uncertainty and aimlessness prepared the soil for the seeds of transformation that would soon be sown.

The turning point in Bob Proctor's life arrived unexpectedly in the early 1960s through a fortuitous encounter with Ray Stanford, a man who saw potential in Proctor that he had not yet recognized. Stanford introduced him to Napoleon Hill's *Think and Grow Rich*, a book that Proctor would read and absorb into the very fabric of his being. The principles outlined in this book—the idea that one's mental attitude directly influences one's ability to succeed—resonated deeply with Proctor. He often recounted that since picking up the book, he read it every day, allowing its philosophies to overhaul his previously entrenched patterns of thinking and acting.

Motivated by Hill's teachings, Proctor started his first venture in the cleaning industry. With no business experience or education beyond high school, he established a cleaning company that remarkably generated over $100,000 in its first year. This initial success was not just a financial win but a practical demonstration of the law of attraction and positive thinking he had learned about from *Think and Grow Rich*. The success of his cleaning business validated his newfound beliefs—it was as if he had discovered a secret key to unlocking a door to a world of potential that he had never imagined could be his to enter.

This early business success began Bob Proctor's lifelong pursuit of learning and teaching success principles. The confidence and knowledge gained from his first business venture enabled him to seek further opportunities for growth and development. He became involved with the Nightingale-Conant organization, a personal development company. He was mentored by Earl Nightingale, another significant influence who further shaped his understanding of human potential.

Bob Proctor's early experiences and struggles shaped not only his character but also his career trajectory. His rise from a high school dropout to a successful businessman and eventually a revered figure in personal development was a direct testament to the principles he later taught to millions. Through his teachings, he would continue to emphasize that everyone, regardless of their background or circumstances, possessed the inner resources to change their life, just as he had. This foundational belief would underpin his future work, making him a beacon of hope and a guide for those seeking to transform their lives.

Philosophical Foundations & Key Teachings

Bob Proctor's teachings were deeply rooted in the Law of Attraction, a principle suggesting that positive or negative thoughts bring positive or negative experiences into a person's life. Proctor's interpretation of this law was not merely philosophical but intensely practical. He believed individuals could manifest their desires through clear intention, visualized goals, and positive thinking. This belief was central to his seminars and written works, where he often demonstrated how a shift in mindset from scarcity to abundance could open doors to limitless possibilities.

In his groundbreaking book, *You Were Born Rich*, Proctor expounds on the idea that everyone possesses innate potential and wealth, which can be activated through awareness and mental reconditioning. The book is a comprehensive guide that explores financial wealth, personal fulfillment, and spiritual richness. It offers strategies such as the concept of the "Image-Maker," a mental faculty Proctor describes as one's ability to visualize and thereby create the necessary conditions for success to manifest in the real world.

The Art of Living is another incredible work that extends his exploration of the metaphysical aspects of success. In this book, Proctor delves into the art of creating a life that's not only successful but also significant. He discusses the importance of aligning one's values and purpose with one's daily actions and decisions, emphasizing that true success comes from a balanced, richly lived experience.

Proctor's mentorship with Earl Nightingale provided a pivotal foundation for his career. Nightingale's influence is evident in Proctor's emphasis on the quality of one's thoughts and their direct correlation with one's quality of life. Nightingale, often considered one of the forefathers of modern personal development, imbued Proctor with a profound responsibility to share these teachings, helping him hone his message and reach a broader audience.

Significant Contributions & Career Highlights

Bob Proctor's career is marked by significant milestones, including his pivotal role in *The Secret*, where he highlighted the practical applications of the Law of Attraction. This appearance helped catapult the concept into mainstream personal development discussions and brought Proctor international fame. His contribution emphasized simplicity in understanding and applying the law, making it accessible and applicable to a global audience.

His teachings on the vibration of thought, the power of affirmations, and the subconscious mind's role in shaping one's reality were revolutionary at the time and remain influential. These concepts were received with mixed reviews—while many embraced them as life-changing, critics often questioned their scientific basis. Nevertheless, Proctor's ability to articulate these ideas in a relatable and actionable way won him millions of adherents worldwide.

Personal Stories & Leadership

Anecdotes from Proctor's life often reflect his leadership qualities and personal philosophy. For instance, carrying and reading *Think and Grow Rich* daily for over 50 years exemplifies his commitment to continuous learning and personal growth. Proctor's leadership style was characterized by his insistence on personal integrity and consistency between one's teachings and life—a principle he lived by unequivocally.

Mentorship & Impact on Others

The Proctor Gallagher Institute, co-founded with Sandy Gallagher, is a testament to his dedication to mentorship and education. The Institute's philosophy is built on Proctor's teachings and is committed to helping individuals use their inherent mental faculties to build fulfilling and prosperous lives. The Institute has impacted thousands through its seminars, publications, and coaching programs, with many participants sharing transformative stories of personal and financial breakthroughs.

Legacy & Continuing Influence

Bob Proctor's legacy in the field of personal development is immense. His work continues to inspire those seeking to understand and utilize the power of their thoughts to achieve more tremendous success and fulfillment. The continued relevance of his teachings is evidenced by the enduring popularity of his books and seminars and the thriving community of practitioners and believers in the principles he championed. His ability to distill complex ideas into practical wisdom ensured that his influence would permeate the field of personal development long after his passing.

Foundational Principles & Truths

At the core of Proctor's teachings were several foundational principles:
- The Law of Attraction
- The Power of Positive Thinking
- The Vital Role of Self-Image

He consistently taught that thoughts are things, a concept that asserts our ability to manifest real-world outcomes through the power of our intentions and beliefs. This idea was central to his philosophy, driving the message that controlling our thoughts can influence our circumstances.

A Literary Legacy: Books that Transformed Lives

Bob Proctor's literary contributions have left an indelible mark on personal development. His most influential book, *You Were Born Rich*, is a comprehensive guide to understanding and harnessing one's innate assets for success and fulfillment. Other notable works include *The Art of Living*, *12 Powerful Principles for Success*, and *The Secret of the Science of Getting Rich*. Each book explores different facets of personal and financial success, providing readers with the tools to transform their lives through renewed thinking and purpose-driven actions.

Philosophy & Self-Image

Proctor emphasized the concept of self-image, teaching that how individuals see themselves fundamentally affects what they can achieve. His philosophy suggested overcoming barriers and achieving unprecedented success by reshaping one's self-image to reflect confidence, competence, and optimism.

Personal & Professional Development

Bob Proctor was a staunch advocate for continuous learning and growth. He emphasized personal development as the cornerstone of professional success, urging his followers to cultivate lifelong learning and self-improvement habits to stay relevant and dynamic in changing environments.

Goals & Success

For Proctor, setting and achieving goals was not just about personal or financial gain but about the growth and satisfaction derived from pursuing something larger than oneself. He taught specific strategies for goal setting and achievement, stressing the importance of clear, actionable objectives paired with strong desire and persistent action.

Mentorship & Beliefs

Mentorship was a critical component of Proctor's philosophy. He believed in the power of guidance from those who have already achieved success, having himself been mentored by greats like Earl Nightingale. His belief system was built around the idea that anyone could achieve greatness with the right guidance and mindset.

A Legacy of Empowerment and Excellence

Bob Proctor's legacy is one of empowerment and excellence. He left behind a body of work and a network of teachings that continue to educate, inspire, and empower individuals worldwide. His methodologies and principles are perpetuated through the Proctor Gallagher Institute, ensuring his mission to uplift lives continues.

The Timeless Principles of Success

Proctor's principles are timeless—centered around the universal laws of success that apply irrespective of time and change. His teachings guide individuals in navigating personal and professional challenges with resilience and wisdom.

Bob Proctor's influence transcends time, with his teachings maintaining relevance in the evolving landscape of personal development. His work inspires new generations, attesting to his insights' enduring appeal and applicability.

Celebrating a Life Well Lived

Bob Proctor passed on February 3, 2022, leaving a legacy that inspires and transforms lives. His life's work celebrated human potential and the belief that everyone has the power to shape their destiny. As we reflect on his contributions, we celebrate a well-lived life marked by profound impacts and timeless teachings that will serve as beacons of hope and transformation for many more years.

~ Habitude Warrior Team ~

ERIK SWANSON

UNLEASHING THE POWER OF MENTORSHIP: A PATHWAY TO UNPARALLELED SUCCESS

"The only limits in our life are those we impose on ourselves."
~ **Bob Proctor**

What an absolute honor it was for me to share many stages with the one and only Bob Proctor! Finding myself learning and growing from the amazing wisdom of Bob Proctor for years upon years, I was pleasantly surprised to be invited to share the stage alongside of Bob at a conference, and then another, and then another. It was meant to be.

I truly embraced the easy going, yet profound way that Bob would teach his audiences. There are many times you will come across brilliant leaders who have ultimate wisdom, yet don't have an approach to allow that wisdom to sink in and stick. Bob was different! He had such a unique way of making everything make sense. He would actually sometimes joke about the fact that common sense isn't that common.

Finding Mentorship in All of the Right Places

In the labyrinth of life, amidst the twists and turns, there exists a beacon of guidance, a guiding light that illuminates the path to success with unwavering clarity. This beacon is none other than mentorship, a profound relationship that transcends time and space, propelling individuals towards their highest aspirations. As Bob Proctor embarked on this journey of enlightenment, I invite you to delve into the transformative power of mentorship, exploring its essence, significance, and the profound impact it holds on personal and professional development.

Unveiling the Essence of Mentorship

Mentorship, dear friends, is not merely a transactional exchange of knowledge; it is a sacred bond forged in the crucible of trust, wisdom, and mutual respect. It embodies the age-old adage, "standing on the shoulders of giants," as mentees glean insights from the experiences and wisdom of their mentors. Mentorship transcends hierarchical boundaries, fostering a symbiotic relationship where both parties embark on a voyage of self-discovery and growth.

At its core, mentorship embodies the essence of guidance, nurturing, and empowerment. A mentor, akin to a seasoned navigator, steers their proteges through the turbulent waters of life, imparting invaluable wisdom garnered through years of trials and triumphs. It is through this symbiotic alliance that individuals transcend their limitations, unlocking the dormant potential that lies within.

Significance of Mentorship in Personal Development

In the tapestry of personal development, mentorship emerges as a cornerstone, laying the foundation for lifelong learning and growth. It is within the hallowed confines of mentorship that individuals are bestowed with the gift of perspective, enabling them to navigate the complexities of life with clarity and conviction.

Through mentorship, individuals embark on a transformative journey of self-discovery, unraveling the intricacies of their innermost desires and aspirations. A mentor, with their keen insight and unwavering support, serves as a catalyst for personal growth, nudging their proteges towards excellence and self-actualization.

Moreover, mentorship fosters resilience and tenacity, instilling within individuals the courage to confront adversity head-on. In the crucible of mentorship, setbacks are reframed as opportunities for growth, propelling individuals towards greater heights of achievement and fulfillment.

Professional Growth & Mentorship

Mentors play a crucial role in personal and professional development for several reasons:

Guidance and Advice: Mentors offer valuable insights and advice based on their own experiences. They can help you navigate challenges, make important decisions, and avoid common pitfalls.

Learning from Experience: A mentor has likely already walked the path you're on and can share their knowledge and lessons learned. This can accelerate your learning curve and help you avoid reinventing the wheel.

Networking Opportunities: Mentors often have extensive networks that they can introduce you to, opening doors to new opportunities, connections, and resources.

Accountability: Having a mentor provides a level of accountability. They can help you set goals, track your progress, and keep you motivated and focused on your objectives.

Encouragement and Support: During times of doubt or difficulty, mentors can provide encouragement, support, and perspective, helping you stay resilient and motivated to overcome challenges.

Personal Growth: Mentors not only help you grow professionally but also personally. They may challenge your assumptions, broaden your perspectives, and encourage you to step outside of your comfort zone.

Ultimately, a mentor serves as a trusted guide and confidant who is invested in your success and development, offering support, wisdom, and encouragement along the way.

The Best Mentors Encourage Your Success

I was truly honored to have lived in a time period where I found myself collaborating with one of the greats of our time. Bob Proctor has changed countless lives around the world, including mine. If you are a student of self-development like I am, then you, too, have decided to devote your time to finding the best of the best around the planet to help catapult your success and to ultimately catapult other's success as well.

The first time I had met Bob Proctor was also the first time I would share the stage with him. What an honor. He is a gentleman, a scholar, and a mentor all wrapped up in to one amazing human.

He took the stage and shared his abundant wisdom and clarity. The audience was in awe of him, as was I. One of my favorite quotes of Bob's is, "The only limits in our life are those we impose on ourselves."

This excited me and scared me at the same time. Excited me because of all of the possibilities that laid in front of me! It scared me also because of all of the possibilities that laid in front of me. I could hear my main mentor, Brian Tracy's voice in my head saying, "You are responsible." This is what I received from Bob in his quote. I received that it truly is up to me… if it's meant to be.

Later that day, I took the stage. And, yes, the audience was once again in awe! I wowed the audience to their core, instilling the belief in them that they, too, can change their own habits and attitudes for the better.

What was so impressive is that Bob Proctor was in the audience as well, watching as I spoke and shared my wisdom and experience. This made me realize what true leaders and mentors do. They are not only there to share, but they are there to learn and grow just like everyone else. A true mentor knows the value of constantly learning from other experts. They take notice and work on their own habits on a daily basis.

I was very impressed!

Later that afternoon, during one of the conference breaks, I headed out to my hotel room to grab my copy of the book *Think and Grow Rich*. This copy was my one and only copy that I had been reading for years. It's the original copy I had ever owned. I found out that Bob started to read *Think and Grow Rich* when he was very young and has read parts of the book every single day since then and has never missed a day.

I was so impressed with this notion that I decided to ask Bob if he would sign my one and only copy of *Think and Grow Rich*. He agreed to do so and signed it for me. He would be the very first person to sign my copy and there started a tradition for me to ask every influential leader and mentor who I share the stage with to also sign my copy of *Think and Grow Rich*.

To this day, I have close to 50 signatures in my copy of the book now. It all started with Bob Proctor impressing me so much and changing not only my life, but the lives of so many around the world. That is a true mentor!

ERIK SWANSON

As an Award-Winning International Keynote Speaker and Multi Time #1 International Best-Selling Author, Erik "Mr. Awesome" Swanson is in great demand around the world! He speaks to an average of more than one million people per year. Mr. Swanson has the honor to have been invited to speak to many schools around the world including the prestigious Harvard University. He is also a recurring Faculty Member of CEO Space International as well as an Alumni Keynoter at Vistage Executive Coaching. Mr. Swanson is also the recipient of 2024's International Book Impact Award and the United States Presidential Lifetime Achievement Award presented by the White House in 2024 for his ongoing community service and philanthropy work. Erik's speeches can be found on Amazon Prime TV as well as joining the Ted Talk Family with his latest speech called, "A Dose of Awesome."

Erik got his start in the self-development world by mentoring directly under Brian Tracy. Quickly climbing to become the top trainer around the world from a group of over 250 handpicked coaches, Erik started to surround himself with the best of the best and very quickly started to be invited to speak on stages alongside such greats as Jim Rohn, Bob Proctor, Les Brown, Sharon Lechter, Jack Canfield, Lisa Nichols, and Joe Dispenza—just to name a few. Erik has created and developed the super-popular Habitude Warrior Conferences and Speaker Hearts Mastermind & Retreats, which have a two-year waiting list and include 33 top-named speakers from around the world. They are 'Ted Talk' style events which have quickly climbed to the top 10 events not to miss in the United States! He is the creator, founder, and CEO of the Habitude Warrior Mastermind, Global Speakers Mastermind, and Cafe Mastermind. He is also the creator and publisher of many book series such as *The 13 Steps To Riches* book series as well as *The Principles of David & Goliath* book series. His motto is clear: "NDSO!": No Drama – Serve Others!

www.SpeakerErikSwanson.com

BRIAN TRACY

MASTERING LEADERSHIP & MENTORSHIP

The world of leadership and mentorship is crucial for anyone aspiring to reach new heights in their professional and personal lives. Through my experiences and the teachings I have shared worldwide, I want to share with you the essential qualities of great leaders and the impactful role of mentorship.

The Essence of Mentorship

Mentorship is a powerful tool for personal and professional development. In my view, to be successful, one absolutely needs to find people who have already paid the price to learn the things that we need to learn. This is the cornerstone of effective mentorship. Whether you are an emerging entrepreneur or a business professional, a mentor can provide guidance, wisdom, and support that is invaluable.

Mentorship, in its most impactful form, exceeds the simple sharing of knowledge—it's a profound relationship that shapes and molds the future through the lens of experience and wisdom. To truly succeed, whether in business or in personal realms, aligning oneself with mentors who have already navigated the complexities of similar paths is essential. These individuals have not only faced the challenges you seek to overcome but have gleaned insights and strategies that only come from real-world experiences. They've paid the price of experience, a price that often involves making mistakes and enduring failures to ultimately forge paths to success.

Consider the journey of an emerging entrepreneur. The landscape of business is fraught with both visible and hidden challenges. A mentor in this context acts not only as a guide but as a strategic advisor. For instance, when I started in the business world, I was fortunate to have mentors who had profound insights into strategic planning and execution. They had the uncanny ability to foresee market trends, identify opportunities, and avoid pitfalls that weren't obvious to the less experienced eye. Their guidance was instrumental in helping me make informed decisions that aligned with long-term objectives, rather than getting sidetracked by short-term gains or distractions.

In professional settings, the role of a mentor is equally invaluable. They provide a sounding board for ideas and decisions, offering feedback that is both encouraging and constructively critical. They help to refine your thoughts, sharpen your focus, and broaden your perspective. For example, in my seminars and coaching sessions, I often share stories of how mentors helped me to see beyond the immediate hurdles and instead focus on what truly matters—building a sustainable and ethical business that delivers real value to its customers.

Moreover, mentorship fosters not just professional growth but personal development. The wisdom imparted by a mentor can help one cultivate qualities such as patience, resilience, and integrity. These are crucial traits that contribute to sustained success but are often overlooked in the fast-paced business environment. My mentors emphasized the importance of these traits, teaching me that success achieved without integrity is no success at all.

Indeed, mentorship can be seen as a catalyst that accelerates the journey towards excellence. It's about more than just achieving goals; it's about expanding what you believe is possible and pushing the boundaries of your own potential. Mentors inspire you, challenge you, and, most importantly, teach you that the path to success is as much about the journey as it is about the destination.

Thus, the heart of mentorship lies in its dual focus on achieving tangible outcomes and fostering personal growth.

Finding the Right Mentor

When looking for a mentor, it's beneficial to start within your own network. This is a resource that is often underutilized but immensely valuable. Look for a mentor who has a positive and well-developed relationship with you, as they are more likely to invest genuinely in your success. If your current network doesn't yield any prospects, then consider expanding your network through professional groups and online platforms like LinkedIn.

Embarking on the search for the right mentor is akin to setting out on a voyage where selecting the right guide can make the difference between reaching your destination successfully or losing your way. The process begins effectively within your own existing network—a resource that is often right under our noses yet frequently overlooked. Your current professional and personal circles are treasure troves of potential mentors. These are individuals who already know you, understand your capabilities, and most importantly, are familiar with your work ethic and personal values. This familiarity forms a solid foundation for a mentorship relationship characterized by trust and mutual respect.

Consider, for example, a former boss, a senior colleague, or even a seasoned professional you've met at industry conferences. These individuals can be pivotal in your development. They already have a sense of your strengths and weaknesses and can provide tailored advice based on real understanding rather than assumptions. One of my first mentors was a senior manager from a previous job. He had observed my work firsthand and could provide specific, actionable guidance that directly impacted my career advancement. His insights helped me not just in tactical decisions, but in shaping my overall career trajectory.

However, what if scanning your immediate network doesn't yield the right mentorship opportunities? This scenario is quite common, and the solution lies in strategically expanding your network. Professional groups, both in-person and online, are excellent venues for meeting experienced individuals who are open to mentoring relationships. Industry-specific forums, professional associations, and networking events provide platforms to connect with potential mentors. Moreover, online platforms like LinkedIn are invaluable tools for reaching out to leaders in your field whom you admire but might not meet in your everyday life.

When utilizing platforms like LinkedIn, approach potential mentors with a clear, respectful message. State why you admire their career path, and specify what aspects of their expertise align with the areas you seek growth in. This approach not only shows your seriousness but also respects the potential mentor's time and achievements.

In expanding your network, consider also the value of diverse perspectives. A mentor from a different industry or background can offer insights that challenge your usual way of thinking and expose you to new methods and strategies. This was exemplified when I sought mentorship from a leader outside my immediate field of expertise, which opened my eyes to innovative management techniques that I had not previously considered. This cross-pollination of ideas was instrumental in developing creative solutions to business challenges.

Remember, the right mentor is not merely someone who gives advice but someone who invests in your success as if it were their own. This kind of relationship requires a genuine connection and a mutual commitment to the growth process. Therefore, starting within your network where existing relationships provide a natural basis for these connections can be very effective. If this isn't an option, then taking proactive steps to broaden your professional circle will increase your chances of finding a mentor who can significantly influence your personal and professional development.

Attending networking events and mastermind groups is another excellent strategy. These gatherings provide a unique opportunity to meet seasoned professionals who can offer mentorship. Remember, the objective is to connect with people who can add value to your professional journey.

In cases where immediate connections aren't available, professional business coaching services may be the solution. These services can offer structured and experienced guidance tailored to your specific career goals. My team and I have provided such mentoring to countless individuals, helping them to accelerate their growth and achieve their most ambitious goals.

Leadership Defined by Key Qualities

Leadership is an art that requires a blend of innate traits and learned skills. Over my career, I've identified several qualities that stand out in all great leaders:

Vision: Great leaders have a clear idea of what they want to accomplish and are excellent at strategic planning. This ability to foresee and articulate the future is what differentiates a leader from a manager.

Courage: Leadership involves taking risks. It requires courage to pursue goals without any guarantee of success. This boldness is a defining characteristic of all great leaders.

Integrity: Perhaps the most important trait of a leader is integrity. It is the foundation of trust and credibility with your team and your stakeholders. Leaders must be honest and transparent in all dealings.

Humility: Effective leadership also involves humility. Leaders must recognize the value of others and admit when they are wrong. This quality fosters respect and loyalty from team members.

Strategic Planning: A leader must be able to look ahead, anticipate changes, and prepare strategically. This not only involves setting goals but also rallying the team to achieve these objectives effectively.

The Impact of Effective Leadership

The ultimate responsibility of a leader is to guide their team towards achieving specific outcomes. By focusing on results and leveraging the strengths of the team, leaders can drive their organizations to success.

This focus on results must be accompanied by an ability to nurture and develop the potential of team members, transforming them into future leaders.

Leadership and mentorship are pivotal in shaping not only the success of individuals but also the cultures and achievements of organizations. Through strategic planning, a commitment to integrity, and fostering a vision for the future, leaders can create a lasting impact.

As we advance in our careers and personal lives, let us strive to embody these qualities of great leaders and mentors. By doing so, we not only enhance our own lives but also contribute positively to the lives of others around us.

I hope you take action and elevate your capabilities in leadership and mentorship. Remember, the journey to excellence is continuous, and with the right mentor and leadership qualities, you are well on your way to achieving your greatest aspirations.

BRIAN TRACY

Brian Tracy is Chairman and CEO of Brian Tracy International, a company specializing in the training and development of individuals and organizations. Brian's goal is to help you achieve your personal and business goals faster and easier than you ever imagined.

Brian Tracy has consulted for more than 1,000 companies and addressed more than 5,000,000 people in 5,000 talks and seminars throughout the US, Canada and 70 other countries worldwide. As a Keynote speaker and seminar leader, he addresses more than 250,000 people each year.

He has studied, researched, written and spoken for 30 years in the fields of economics, history, business, philosophy and psychology. He is the Top-Selling Author of over 70 books that have been translated into dozens of languages.

He has written and produced more than 300 audio and video learning programs, including the worldwide, best-selling *Psychology of Achievement*, which has been translated into more than 28 languages.

He speaks to corporate and public audiences on the subjects of Personal and Professional Development, including the executives and staff of many of America's largest corporations. His exciting talks and seminars on Leadership, Selling, Self-Esteem, Goals, Strategy, Creativity and Success Psychology bring about immediate changes and long-term results. Brian Tracy is the recipient of many prestigious awards including The Habitude Warrior Lifetime Achievement Award for excellence, The Los Angeles Tribune Lifetime Achievment Award, and The Cathcart Institute Certified Professional Expert Award.

Brian Tracy is an active contributor to Speaker Hearts International assisting aspiring speakers to find their voices and share their hearts through community service and philanthropic efforts (*www.SpeakerHearts.com*). He has traveled and worked in over 107 countries on six continents, and speaks four languages. Brian is happily married and has four children. He is active in community and national affairs, and is the President of three companies headquartered in Solana Beach, California.

www.BrianTracy.com

BARBARA MAJESKI

THE BEST STUDENT IN A CLASS OF WINNING

In middle school, my dad drove us around beautiful neighborhoods to see these magnificent mansions. We would ooh and aah over and over again about the magnificence of their landscaping, their driveways, and their cars. From time to time, he would also take us to Ferrari dealerships to pick out what kind of Ferrari Testarossa we wanted.

All the while, we struggled to keep a roof over our heads, our mode of transportation was a painter's van with only two seats, and our food budget, being generous enough, could only include $0.99 meals at Denny's. Financially, we struggled.

I'm the only girl out of four kids and the oldest of two sets of twins. My twin brother is Ben, and my two younger twin brothers are Michael and Steven. Twins run in our family, as my mom is a triplet. So does Fragile X, a genetically inherited form of neurological impairment. Steven has a fragile X. So, from an early age, I always assumed that, as the girl of the family, I would be his caretaker. No one asked me to be his caretaker. I just assumed it.

So, on this one particular day, my dad takes us to the Ferrari dealership, and on the way home, I start hysterically crying. I was a 13-year-old girl living with her three brothers, her uncle, and her dad in a one-bedroom studio apartment in La Jolla, California. Yeah, a meltdown was in order.

So, we pulled into the apartment complex, and my dad and I stood outside in the parking lot.

I could not reconcile why we were going to pick out Ferraris and look at giant mansions when we were living with his brother and driving in a two-seater van. I saw the price tags were well above our means, and I didn't understand this form of torture. I just wanted a car with seats.

My dad made it very simple for me" Someone else buys these cars and these homes. We need to learn what they did to get what they have and do the same thing.

And that has been my formula for success. Do what they do and get what they have. Good things, bad things, or ugly things... you choose through your actions your results. Do the things to get the things.

Knowing that I have a brother with special needs who could never care for himself, I made it my mission to ensure I had enough wealth and resources to provide for him. At an early age, I recognized that to provide for him, I needed to make money—not just get paid but build a robust nest egg. So that is what I've spent my life doing ... studying and mastering how people save and develop generational wealth.

Fortunately, my dad's equation was straightforward and one that I could easily follow. And now I'm passing it on to you.

Find people that have what you want. And do what they do. He never mentioned anything about birthright or luck or "being gifted." It was all about taking action. Do the things. Fortunately, I never said anything about being a good SAT academic or athlete. His message was to me: work hard at the right things, and you'll get the results.

Here's what I've spent my life doing: Find the right mentors, coaches, and examples. Follow their lead. It's a cut-and-paste strategy that has worked exceptionally well for me.

I found books for the first time that launched me into personal wealth development. I studied Rick Pitino, Tony Robbins, and even Donald

Trump (his books were good, and it was the 90's). Those were my first mentors. Eventually, I would find my way to get seats at good tables, surround myself with good people, and align myself with thought leaders, pioneers, and go-getters.

The mistake I see people make repeatedly is they get advice from people who have yet to learn what they're talking about. But just because somebody has your best interest at heart doesn't mean they know what is best. Unless they are where you want to be, they are not the people to ask directions from. I learned early: Do not seek counsel where you seek comfort.

Take my dad's advice. Find people who inspire, motivate, and educate you—people who spark your curiosity and nurture your eagerness to grow and learn. Mentorship can come in the form of a book or a podcast as you embark on your personal growth and development. That is where I started. Eventually, it was finding the right tables to sit at, places to be, people to talk to, and so on.

I have learned that the right experienced mentor has perspective and insights you likely lack on your own. They can see your untapped potential and guide you in fulfilling it. A good mentor challenges you to grow into the most robust version of yourself.

With their mentorship, you'll waste less time on activities that don't align with your goals. You'll discover work you find meaningful and rewarding. With their advice, you can turn your dreams into realities. Take my dad's advice: Find someone who inspires you and become the best student in their class of winning.

BARBARA MAJESKI

Barbara Majeski is a force to be reckoned with, embodying strength, resilience, and an insatiable zest for life. Known as the "Curator of the Good Life," Barbara's journey to this title was far from easy-it was forged through the trials of motherhood, a life-altering cancer diagnosis, and a flourishing career as an on-air television personality. Her visibility and impact have been widespread. She's been live on the plaza with the TODAY Show multiple times and has traveled the globe, finding love and prospering on her own terms along the way.

A savvy investor and self-challenger, Barbara has learned the art of walking away from things, people, and situations that don't serve her well-being. Her television appearances are numerous, extending beyond the *TODAY Show* to platforms like *Inside Edition, Fox, Good Day New York*, and many more, always embodying her role as "The Curator of the Good Life." But what does it mean to be the "Curator of the Good Life?" For Barbara, it's not just about relishing the luxe and opulence that the world has to offer. It's a philosophy that calls for embracing each moment, be it joyful or challenging, and using those life experiences to cultivate a life teeming with style, purpose, and adventure.

Her unique brand of authenticity has earned her the moniker "The Queen of Oversharing." Barbara pulls no punches when it comes to sharing the highs and lows of her personal journey. Whether she's live on the plaza with the *TODAY Show* or dishing out "Steals and Deals," her aim is singular: to inspire her audience to overcome their own hurdles, to venture outside their comfort zones, and to discover their personal version of the good life.

www.BarbaraMajeski.com

PAUL BLANCHARD

THE RIPPLE EFFECTS OF PROFOUND MENTORSHIP

Mentorship has been around for over 3,000 years. Arguably, it is one of the most powerful developments in advancing society, technology, and more. Throughout history, we see great minds, inventors, and leaders shaped by mentorship. In some cultures, it is a communal practice woven into the fabric of society. In more modern settings, mentorship is often overshadowed by commercial coaching and incentivized leadership programs. While these have merit, there remains an important and distinct role for mentorship.

Regardless of whether mentorship is actively sought or naturally present, it is an essential ingredient for accelerated growth and self-actualization. At its core, what is a mentor beyond a guide, advisor or witness who embodies the patience we cannot yet summon alone? The vision, strategy, and improvement we may seek from a mentor are all enhanced by their wisdom to go slow.

One of my favorite examples of mentorship is Glinda from The Wizard of Oz. When Dorothy finds herself displaced, disoriented, and in unfamiliar territory, it is Glinda who helps her find her way. This timeless tale exemplifies many of the key facets of impactful mentorship.

Seeking Out Mentors

Great mentors often appear when we are filleted wide open by life's turbulence and realize brute force is not the answer. The old saying goes, "When the student is ready, the teacher appears." In truth, readiness may be less about resolve and more about realizing our usual tools are insufficient for the task or trials at hand.

We must also be open to mentors who do not fit our preconceived notions. Dorothy did not expect a good witch dressed like Glinda. Yet there she was, a helper Dorothy nearly missed. When we find ourselves out of our element, the first step toward mentorship is simply stepping out and stepping forward from where we've been planted (not buried). But we must not cling to old ways and assumptions that no longer serve us. Be open to mentors who look, sound or act differently than anticipated.

Discerning Needs vs. Wants

In crisis, our vision narrows to solve the immediate challenge. Returning home was Dorothy's singular focus upon landing in Oz. She asked Glinda for just that—to go home. But a wise mentor understands the presenting request may not address underlying needs. Rather than solve Dorothy's problem outright, Glinda provided a path for discovery—the Yellow Brick Road.

Great mentors are not problem solvers. They know their solutions may not fit our journey. The greatest gift is creating space for the mentee to explore, reveal and discover with gentle guidance when needed. Mentorship is not about transplanting the mentor's experiences and lessons. We must each walk our own Yellow Brick Road, learning from the trees that throw apples, the people with more heart or courage than expected, those pretending to have all the answers, and even our own insecurities that seem to sabotage progress.

I once insisted a business mentor get me out of a jam and point me to a solution. But his restraint allowed space for my own strategy to organically emerge and even more importantly the wherewithal to sustain it. I discovered solutions tailored to my strengths that no amount of advice could have crafted.

Through this journey of wins, wounds and revelations, mentors support and witness our unfolding. Their steadfast presence builds trust in our own inner wisdom. In time, the mentee comes home—not to a physical place, but to a sense of belonging within.

The Mentor-Mentee Dance

Mentorship is a dance requiring two willing partners. The mentee will want to bring humility, dedication, and sincere curiosity about the relationship. Listen fully. Apply counsel to action. Let your mentor witness your growth—it is life's greatest reward. Offer your own insights in return through courageous dialogue. Conclude by sharing your progress and profound gratitude.

And mentors will want to respond with deep care, guiding firmly yet allowing self-direction. Gently stretch abilities. Share hard-won lessons. Model values and healthy boundaries while inspiring mentees to live theirs boldly. Showcase new horizons while encouraging the mentee's style of mastery. The mentor-mentee relationship is temporary yet eternally impactful when danced with care.

I will never forget Tracy Callahan, my theater director in college. She challenged me to grasp nuance, connect at a soul level, and think critically deeper than the surface. I carried those lessons long after my college experience. Years later, I have become a mentor to others as she did for me. That is mentorship's endless chain.

The Ripple Effects

Mentorship sets an endless chain of guidance in motion. All of us stand on the shoulders of those who shaped our growth. My love of learning and unapologetic expression traces back to Mrs. Call in 3rd grade. She saw a spark and fanned it to flames. I write and speak today because she empowered me to embrace my voice.

When the time comes, may we pay this profound gift forward. Let us each become the listening ear, the gentle push, and the wise mirror for others still learning to trust their inner voice. For the mentor-mentee journey continues forever, one understanding heart and hand reaching out to the next. There is no greater mission.

Sparking the Cycle Anew

How do we spark this cycle anew? First, recall those who mentored you. Send a note sharing the impact they made. Let them witness the fruit they nurtured. Then act. Even small actions plant seeds of mentorship.

We all have wisdom to share, especially with those earlier on the journey. But mentorship works both ways. There is often much to learn from those we perceive as less experienced. Stay open to reverse mentoring opportunities as well.

I hope these thoughts ignite your mentor spirit. Small actions plant seeds that grow into towering trees of guidance. And you never know whose life you'll change. So, begin today—for the ripple effects of mentorship last forever.

PAUL BLANCHARD

Paul Blanchard stands out in the realms of business coaching, executive mentoring, and transformative speaking. With over 15 years of dedicated expertise, Paul has distinguished himself as a pioneering Executive & Entrepreneur Coach and a Somatic Mapmaker, deeply committed to the holistic development of business leaders and individuals seeking profound personal and professional growth.

As the founder of Whole Body Mindset, Paul has meticulously designed an innovative approach that synthesizes personal development, somatic integration, and cognitive enhancement with strategic life and business planning. This unique methodology is grounded in rigorous scientific research, extensive mathematical analysis, and hands-on application across various industries. His signature coaching style is anything but conventional, catering to real people facing real challenges, and providing solutions that are both practical and transformative.

Paul's professional journey includes remarkable accomplishments such as contributing to the creation of a Top-25 Executive MBA program alongside the iconic CEO Jack Welch. His deep dive into the neurological patterns of entrepreneurs and executives through the science of Axiology has impacted thousands, including major corporations like Boeing and Microsoft.

His tenure as President of Habit Finder has been marked by significant achievements, where he has guided thousands of individuals and organizations to disrupt unhelpful behavioral patterns, reigniting their passion and elevating their professional lives. The proprietary Habit Finder technology, which Paul utilizes, has helped streamline the path to deeper insights by scientifically measuring the subconscious habits that govern behavior.

Among his accolades, Paul has received the Corporate Excellence Award from Strayer University, linked to his impactful work at the Jack Welch Management Institute, and a Brand Ambassador Award for his pivotal role in enhancing operational strategies and performance.

Currently, Paul continues to expand his impact through Whole Body Mindset, embracing a remote, global platform to reach and transform a wider audience. His work is a testament to his belief in the potential of every individual to find and leverage their inner strengths, redefining what they can achieve in business and in life.

Paul's commitment extends beyond individual coaching to large-scale engagements where he speaks and facilitates workshops that are tailored to resonate and catalyze change in everyone from small team gatherings to large corporate assemblies.

Through his innovative methods and dedicated coaching, Paul Blanchard continues to be a beacon of change, helping individuals and organizations to not only envision a better future but to actively create it.

www.WholeBodyMindset.com

"THOUGHTS BECOME THINGS. IF YOU SEE IT IN YOUR MIND, YOU WILL HOLD IT IN YOUR HAND."

~ BOB PROCTOR

AMY KEIDERLING

LIFE IS NOW

. . . .

It was St. Patty's Day—March 17th, 2020—and it was the day that my life changed forever—for the better. It is a day that I say I got lucky for many reasons. Not only is it the date that I met my soul mate and life partner, but it was a day that I received "the call" that no one wants to answer. That's right—"THE CALL." Now, this is not your normal telemarketing call, or a child calling to say they forgot their lunch, or a friend in need of unloading all her stresses. This is the call that stops you dead in your tracks and marks the point where your life is forever changed.

My call came while celebrating Keith and I's anniversary in a Mexican restaurant. It was the call that said, "You Have Cancer." We had been anxiously waiting for the biopsy results from a routine mammogram. I have had suspicious mammograms in the past, but this time it was different. There was this gut instinct, intuition or spiritual nudge that told me this was not going to be the same.

I had been mentally preparing myself as I had been the cancer caregiver for several friends and family members over the years. I knew the process, what items to put in the chemo bag, how to ask the right questions and how long this battle was going to take.

"YOU GOT THIS AMY" was what I silently cheered to myself over and repeatedly—convincing myself to stay positive and optimistic despite every ounce in my body was screaming differently.

Now, one would naturally assume that since the cancer was found during a routine mammogram it was a breast cancer diagnosis...NOPE! I can still feel the shock and disbelief rush over my body when they doctor explained that I did not have breast cancer and instead she explained that I had lymphoma.

WHAT? I remember my head spinning and immediately searching my past database of science classes and getting angry I had not paid more attention. LYMPHOMA? Lymphoma? LYMPHOMA! My brain was not processing the word and the first thing that came out of my mouth was, "So I am not getting new boobs?" The silence on the other end of the line was deafening and what seemed like forever before the doctor came back and said, "No, it's a blood cancer."

Now wait a minute—and then it clicked—LLS or the Leukemia Lymphoma Society! I had been supporting and raising money for them for years. I suddenly went from cancer caregiver to cancer patient with "the call."

"The Call" started us on a wild journey as we navigated cancer, Covid, our businesses being shut down due to travel bans and our retail store closing—all resulting in no income. I had always heard of people hitting rock bottom, and I have been through a lot of "life lessons" in my past, but this was the BIG ONE! Our journey discovered that my official diagnosis was Stage IV Non-Hodgkins Follicular Lymphoma.

That's right—Stage IV and it was throughout my entire body and in my bones. The cancer had surrounded every major organ and during my PET scan I lit up like a Christmas Tree showing the cancer. We started on the long road of endless tests, scans, biopsies, doctors, nurses, blood draws, appointments, and many hours in Lazy Boy Lounge receiving and praying that this bag of liquids would be the answer.

Non-Hodgkin's Follicular Lymphoma does not have a cure...yet. I will never be able to say that I beat cancer (yet), and instead I say that I beat it down. Our goal is to knock it down away from any major organs or arteries to ensure longevity of life. So basically—I will die with this until a cure is found as it continues to grow. Still thinking I got lucky?

I am forever grateful and blessed for those two evil twin sisters: Cancer and Covid. They came into my life and forced me to slow down, appreciate every single moment and cherish the ones that I love. They have also brought into my life amazing people from doctors, nurses, spiritual guides, and mentors, all whom I never would have crossed paths with without them. They have brought me consciously aware of amazing authors, set my course on self-improvement and empowering myself to change my mindset and create my outcome.

I was not meant to be a sacrifice and I knew at that moment that I was up to big things and there was a purpose. Life was happening for me and not to me. We were able to knock down the cancer and started our new "normal" of every 90 days doc checks…lucky me!

Guess what!?! In May of 2022, that darn phone ran again! That's right, I got "the call" again. I know you are probably thinking by now, "Stop answering the phone." The cancer had woken up. That's right—it decided to wake up in my stomach with multiple tumors. One of the side effects of my cancer is extreme weight loss, but NOPE, didn't get lucky there. No boobs and no weight loss. A sign from the universe that there are greater lessons in store for me.

When this call came, it was different. I was in the middle of an amazing emotional intelligence program, I was finally getting to know the real authentic me, and I had met some amazing individuals and mentors. I did not have time for Round 2. I had things to do and people to see. I chose to postpone treatment until after the class was over—until an amazing woman and mentor powerfully and lovingly asked me why. Now she not only was curious, but she asked the one question that no one close to me could bear to ask: "Why wait?"

She then spoke three very powerful words that I have now embraced as my motto for life: LIFE IS NOW! Life is happening for us and not to us. Each day we are faced at the crossroads in our journey called life. We can powerfully choose to live in the present moment and make the most of one's circumstances or we can choose to avoid and life in fear. I got lucky in meeting my mentor, Elaine. It's incredible to find someone who unapologetically authentically sees you for who you be and will hold you high to allow you to see your greatness that has always been inside. I powerfully stood at that choice line and decided that LIFE IS NOW, and I opted for treatment or round 2. And we knocked it down again!

Now, you may be still questioning why I say that "the call" was the day I got lucky. The gifts, people, experiences, memories, inspiration, empowerment, mentoring and spiritual awakenings that the "twins" have gifted me is priceless. Guess what?!? As I was blessed with this opportunity to share a little bit about my journey and LIFE IS NOW, my phone rang. That's right, I just got "the call." I just got lucky, and I bet you can guess what my decision will be for round 3.

LIFE IS NOW! LIFE IS NOW! LIFE IS NOW!

AMY KEIDERLING

About Amy Keiderling: Amy Keiderling is a Rebel Soul Guide. She helps to navigate you to find your soul's purpose. Think of her as a co-pilot on the road of life. When the road gets bumpy, curvy, or just seems full of obstacles and detours, we will pull out our Rebel Roadmap and navigate it together.

Amy Keiderling is the owner of Rebel Roadmap, MOdville, as well as an adventure guide with MO Adventures. Amy has always been an avid collector of anything vintage; the instant connection a piece gives you to a memory or story is why she loves her fab finds & and creating memories. Amy's passion grew stronger when she met Keith, as his passion for custom vintage cars, motorcycles, and random collectibles grew their collection. When Amy and Keith are not taking adventure lovers on chartered vacations/ retreats, or riding around on their motorcycles, you will find them lounging in the middle of MOwhere on their 30-acre Mid-Century Modern Retreat Property. LIFE IS NOW! Amy's battle cry - as she's experienced life from everything from divorce, body image struggles, self-worth, bankruptcy, food stamps, single parenthood, starting 4 businesses, being a Rock Star Mom & Mimi to her Bigs & Littles, and a cancer warrior fighting Non-Hodgkin's Lymphoma! Amy's road may be "bumpy", but she's grateful for her "off road" adventure called LIFE. Amy encourages everyone to navigate their road of life and follow their inner GPS full of MO Adventures, MO Fun & MO Memories with the ones you love.

Author's Website: *www.ItsAMoAdventure.com* & *www.RebelRoadmap.com* *@RebelRoadmap*

Book Series Website: *www.TheBookOfMentors.com*

DR. ANGELA HARDEN-MACK, MD

YOU HAVE THE POWER TO CREATE YOUR DREAM LIFE

Have you ever wondered why some people seem to effortlessly attract good fortune and opportunity while others struggle to get ahead no matter how hard they try? The answer lies not in our outward circumstances or even our actions alone, but in our inner world of thoughts. Our thoughts define our reality, for better or for worse, because they shape our beliefs which then determine our choices and therefore our destiny.

This might sound like nothing more than hopeful rhetoric, but the truth is there is immense power locked in the hidden recesses of our mind that we have barely even begun to understand, let alone wield for our highest good. I'm delighted to share with you some profound yet practical insights from personal development legend Bob Proctor on how to harness the hidden power of your thoughts to create the life you truly desire. By understanding three of Proctor's quotes based on Laws of Manifestation, you will learn to escape the trap of self-limiting thoughts and beliefs that hold so many back, and instead cultivate an unstoppable mindset that attracts opportunity and success like a magnet.

I hope these teachings ignite a fire of inspiration and possibility within you to go out each day and build the future of your dreams. Read on to gain life-changing insights that will light your path to unlimited success.

If you believe in the power of your thoughts to manifest abundance in your life, you have the ability to create the life you desire. Looking for an example of a life created using manifestation? Gain inspiration from Bob Proctor, a prime example of how understanding universal laws and applying them in daily life can lead to incredible success. Proctor, like many other successful people, attributes his breakthrough to his discovery of the power of thought in Napoleon Hill's classic book, *Think and Grow Rich*. With a deep understanding of the three laws of manifestation—the Law of Belief, Outer Correspondence, and the Law of Attraction—Proctor became a master of manifestation.

You, too, can learn to create an abundant life by understanding and applying these laws. Don't wait for success to come to you, take control of your thoughts and manifest the life you desire.

The power of our thoughts is undeniable. It's what drives us, motivates us, and shapes our reality. And when it comes to the universal laws, the Law of Belief holds a special place. It's the foundation upon which the Law of Attraction and the Law of Vibration rest. Believing in yourself, your abilities, and the infinite possibilities that exist in the universe is essential if you want to manifest your dreams into reality. As Bob Proctor once said, "Don't expect a great day; create one." And that's exactly what the Law of Belief allows us to do. It empowers people to take control of their thoughts, to tap into their inner strength, and to create the life they desire. Because when you truly believe, the universe opens up, and the magic of manifestation begins.

The Law of Outer Correspondence may sound like some complicated scientific theory, but it's actually a simple, yet powerful, concept that can revolutionize the way we live our lives. Imagine having the power to intentionally create the life that you want, just by changing the thoughts and beliefs that you hold within yourself. Because, as the law states, your outer world is a reflection of your inner world. This means that your self-talk, the beliefs you hold, and the way you perceive the world is what shapes your reality.

The Law of Belief and other universal laws teach us that we have the ability to manifest our desires into reality, but it all starts with the inner world. So, if you're feeling stuck or unsatisfied with your life, remember that you have the power to create the changes you seek. It's time to take control of your thoughts and beliefs, and watch as your outer world begins to transform accordingly.

The Law of Attraction is one of the most potent and well-known universal laws that govern how we attract and repel things in our lives. The power of attraction is compelling; it shapes our environment, our relationships, our experiences, and our life. Attraction happens whether or not you are aware of it. It is not just about positive thinking; it is about creating the energy of what you want to manifest in your life.

When people learn to use this powerful and essential law effectively, they understand the art of manifestation. The key is to keep your thoughts, emotions and intentions focused on the good things in your life and being grateful for them. The Law of Attraction is a powerful tool that helps people create the life they want.

Manifestation is not merely a concept; it's a dynamic tool that has fueled real happiness and success for me. While the Law of Attraction is undoubtedly impactful, I resonate profoundly with the Law of Outer Correspondence. This law says that our external world mirrors our internal world, and to induce change, mastery over our thoughts, emotions, beliefs, and self-talk is crucial.

Empowerment lies in taking control of your life. My core belief—that all things are possible if you believe—is paired with the powerful thought, "I am an Awesome Achiever, and I am living my dreams." The emotion of joy propels my success, and my "power" words, "I love you Angela, and I believe in you," serve as a daily affirmation that I can create the life I desire. Let's master the universal laws of manifestation to attract what we desire and repel what we don't.

In the world we live in, it's easy to get caught up in negative thoughts and fears. But as Bob Proctor has taught us, our thoughts have the power to shape our reality. By understanding and applying three laws of manifestation, we can harness the immense power of our thoughts and create a life beyond our wildest dreams.

It may not be easy, but it is certainly worth it. Imagine waking up every day to a life filled with love, abundance, and fulfillment—that could be your reality if you choose to think positively and manifest your desires. So, don't let your doubts and fears hold you back any longer. Start by shifting your mindset and focusing on what you truly want from life. Remember, you are capable of achieving anything you set your mind to. Take control of your thoughts and create your own destiny starting today!

As Bob Proctor says, "Thoughts become things." And with that knowledge at hand, it's time for you to start manifesting the life you deserve. Believe in yourself, believe in the power of thought, and watch as your dreams become a reality before your very eyes. You got this!

DR. ANGELA HARDEN-MACK, MD

About Dr. Angela Harden-Mack, MD: Dr. Angela Harden-Mack, MD, is a woman on a mission serving ambitious success-oriented career women. Dr. Angela uses her keynote to motivate women to take action to release the stressful and pressured Superwoman lifestyle to be healthier and happier enjoying personal and professional success. Dr. Angela, wellness expert, women's empowerment coach, international speaker, and entrepreneur, has been featured in print and broadcast media.

Learn more about Dr. Angela and her company, Live Great Lives, at *www.DrAngela360.com*.

Author's Website: *www.LiveGreatLives.com*

Book Series Website: *www.TheBookOfMentors.com*

AZADEH BENNETT

HOW TO KNOW THEY ARE THE RIGHT MENTOR

"A mentor is someone who sees more talent and ability within you, than you see in yourself, and helps bring it out of you."
~ **Bob Proctor**

My First & Greatest Mentor

In the tapestry of life, every individual thread is guided by hands that shape its direction, color, and texture. Among these guiding hands, mentors hold a pivotal role, embodying the essence of Bob Proctor's wisdom: "A mentor is someone who sees more talent and ability within you, than you see in yourself, and helps bring it out of you." Reflecting upon this truth, I recognize the indelible mark of my first and greatest mentor—my father.

From my earliest memories, my father was the luminary in the darkness, the one who saw the uncharted potential within me. In a world that often settles for the surface, he perceived depths in me that I had yet to discover. He was not just a parent; he was my thought leader, the architect of my curiosity, and the catalyst for my undying interest in the vast expanse of science and the universe.

I fondly recall our nocturnal journeys, where the car became our vessel navigating through the night, and the sky above us a canvas of mysteries waiting to be unraveled. As my mother tasked me with keeping my father company during those drives, our conversations would take flight into the realms of stars, black holes, and galaxies. His patience was the bridge that connected my eager mind to the cosmos, fueling my wonder and thirst for knowledge.

His influence didn't wane as I grew older. When the crossroads of my academic journey beckoned, it was his gentle nudge that steered me towards Tehran University, Iran's apex of academic excellence. Mathematics, a discipline I approached with trepidation, became my chosen path.

Despite my reservations, he believed in my capacity to excel, to endure, and to emerge triumphant. His belief was not anchored in blind faith but in a profound understanding of my potential—a potential that I was yet to see in myself.

Financial constraints might have limited his support to encouragement and moral guidance, yet it was his vision that planted the seed of ambition in my heart—a vision that transcended the boundaries of our circumstances. The idea of going abroad, of expanding my horizon beyond the familiar landscapes of Iran, was his gift to me. He instilled in me the belief that I was destined for more than the ordinary, not out of disdain for simplicity but out of recognition of the fire that burned within me. He taught me that with passion and perseverance, the possibilities were boundless.

To be ordinary is to be part of the fabric of life, a beautiful existence in its own right. However, my father's teachings revealed to me that my thread was woven with a different pattern, a pattern that was meant to stretch beyond the conventional, to impact the world in ways I had yet to comprehend. This realization was his legacy to me—a legacy of empowerment, resilience, and unyielding curiosity.

My father, the first and greatest mentor I ever had, laid the foundation for who I am today. His lessons transcended the academic and entered the realm of the existential, teaching me the value of questioning, exploring, and reaching for the stars, both literally and metaphorically. For this, I am eternally grateful.

"Baba," the gift of life you gave me was more than just existence; it was a journey illuminated by the light of your wisdom and love. Your legacy lives on, not just in the memories we share, but in every step I take forward, guided by the lessons you've instilled in me.

Envisioning a Dream: The Journey from Visualization to Reality

The Power of Visualization

My journey of self-discovery and realization began with a profound statement from Bob Proctor: "Thoughts become things. If you see it in your mind, you will hold it in your hand." This quote resonated with me at a deep level.

I recall vividly how, years before I set foot in the United States, I visualized myself there. These visualizations, akin to prayers, were my way of asking for divine guidance and support in my endeavor, to not rely on applying for the Diversity Visa Lottery but put my effort into finding other ways to come to the US. I chose to come as a student.

Discovering Purpose

After embracing my new life here in the US for Over ten years, my focus shifted to finding my purpose. Inspired by Brian and Gabrielle Bosche's insights in the book, *The Purpose Factor*, I delved into the questions: Who am I? Whom am I meant to serve? My exploration through personality tests and human design charts revealed that I am creative, visionary, strategist, fun, and connected.

My vision is to bridge people globally through love, communication, and creativity. My big vision in life is to bring the legends and mythical stories of the book of *Shahnameh*, from ancient Persia, to life through animation and connect the world with Persia, the first civilization in the world.

The Shahnameh: A Beacon of Persian Cultural Heritage

The Shahnameh Vision

In the heart of Persian literature lies *The Shahnameh*, the Epic Book of the Persian Kings, an unparalleled masterpiece that has withstood the test of time. Authored by the esteemed poet, Abolghasem Ferdowsi, this work is not just a book; it is a cultural treasure trove, a beacon of resilience, and a testament to the enduring spirit of the Persian people.

Ferdowsi's dedication to crafting this epic in poetic literature over three decades, during a tumultuous era when Persians faced immense pressure to abandon their language and culture in favor of adopting Islam and Arabic, speaks volumes about the importance of preserving one's heritage.

The Shahnameh's significance in Persian culture and history cannot be overstated. It is a poetic compendium that intricately weaves together the myths, legends, and history of Persia. This epic stands as a bastion of the Persian language and identity, serving as a defiant response to the cultural erosion threatened by the Arab invasion. Ferdowsi's genius lay in his ability to encapsulate the essence of an entire civilization within the bounds of poetry, ensuring that the Persian language and its rich history were not only preserved but celebrated.

Beyond its historical and linguistic importance, *The Shahnameh* is a masterclass in storytelling. It brings to life a myriad of characters, from heroic figures and malevolent adversaries to complex personalities, each contributing to the rich tapestry of Persian mythology. These stories are more than mere tales; they are the collective memory of a nation, a moral compass that has guided generations, and a source of inspiration for countless artists, writers, and thinkers.

Moreover, *The Shahnameh* transcends its role as a historical document. It embodies the timeless themes of heroism, justice, love, and the eternal struggle between good and evil. These universal themes resonate beyond the boundaries of time and geography, making the epic relevant even in contemporary times. The work's ability to inspire, educate, and entertain is a testament to its enduring appeal.

In my vision to bring *The Shahnameh* to life through animation, I aim to not only honor this monumental work but also to introduce it to new audiences worldwide. By translating these ancient stories into a modern medium, I aspire to share the rich Persian heritage and its timeless tales with a global audience. This project is more than just an adaptation; it is a bridge connecting the past with the present, the East with the West, and traditional storytelling with contemporary art forms.

The journey of animating *The Shahnameh* is not just about preserving a piece of literature; it's about keeping alive the spirit of a culture that has faced challenges yet continues to thrive. It's about showing the world the resilience, beauty, and depth of Persian civilization. Through this endeavor, I aim to inspire others to explore and appreciate the diverse and rich cultural landscapes that shape our world.

Dreaming in Animation

My aspiration to create animation was kindled when I first watched *The Little Mermaid* in middle school. The magical storytelling through animation captivated me, and I dreamed of merging computer engineering with this art form. Life, however, took me down different academic paths—mathematics, and business—leaving my animation dream seemingly out of reach. But the vision of bringing *The Shahnameh* to life through animation, akin to Walt Disney's quality, remains a burning ambition.

Embracing the Journey

Bob Proctor once said, "Anyone that ever accomplished anything, did not know how they were going to do it. They only knew they were going to do it." This quote is a beacon as I embark on the daunting yet exhilarating journey to animate, *The Shahnameh*. The magnitude of this project aligns perfectly with another of Proctor's insights: "If your goal isn't scary and exciting, then it's not a big enough goal for you." This project, indeed, is both.

The Inner Strength

In moments of doubt, I remind myself of Proctor's words: "There is no problem outside of you that is superior to the power within you." This affirmation, along with, "You have within you right now, everything you need to deal with whatever the world can throw at you," bolsters my resolve. It underlines the belief that I am the master of my destiny, a notion echoed in Proctor's assertion that we can influence, direct, and control our environment.

As I give myself a 10 to 15-year timeline to realize this dream, I invite those who know me to be part of this journey. Your support, encouragement, and engagement are not just appreciated but essential. Together, we can share this precious vision with the world, proving that with belief, vision, and relentless pursuit, even the most ambitious dreams can become reality.

In conclusion, my story is a testament to Bob Proctor's philosophy that the power of our thoughts, coupled with action, can shape our destiny. From a visualization years ago to the steps I am taking today, I am living proof that if you can see it in your mind and work towards it, you can indeed hold it in your hand.

AZADEH BENNETT

About Azadeh Bennett: Azadeh Bennett, a dynamic creative leadership consultant and transformational coach, Author and speaker, is a fervent advocate for "woman life freedom," tirelessly championing the rights of women globally. Armed with master's degrees in MBA, Strategic Communication, and Global Studies, she is dedicated to empowering individuals on their journey to personal and professional growth.

Azadeh's unwavering dedication is complemented by her loving marriage to Jason Bennett, whose steadfast support fuels her passion for transformation and freedom. Together, they embody the power of love and partnership in pursuing one's life purpose.

Beyond her professional endeavors, Azadeh finds solace in nature through hiking and expresses her creativity by playing the harp and painting with acrylics. Her commitment to fostering creativity, leadership, freedom, and communication shines through in her work with individuals and organizations.

Moreover, Azadeh is a visionary strategist who excels in connecting people through love and creating joyous experiences. Her remarkable vision to visualize Shahnameh in animation and share it with the world showcases her profound cultural intelligence and communication skills, enriching global understanding and appreciation for Persian culture.

Author's Website: *www.AzadehBennett.com*

Book Series Website: *www.TheBookofMentors.com*

DR. BETTY SPEAKS
GUIDING WINGS

The Transformative Power of Focus in Leadership and Mentorship

In the realm of leadership and mentorship, the significance of staying focused cannot be overstated. My story is about a remarkable individual whose life story serves as an inspiration and exemplifies the power of focus in achieving dreams. From my childhood fantasies of flying away to the real-life hand-gliding adventure in Europe, my journey emphasizes the importance of staying focused, especially when navigating unfamiliar territories.

Childhood Dream

As a child, I harbored dreams of soaring away from home, much like a bird escaping its nest. Little did I know that these childhood fantasies would manifest in a tangible and awe-inspiring way later in life. This biographical element provides a poignant backdrop to our exploration of the importance of focus in leadership and mentorship.

As we navigate through the narrative of life, we often find that our childhood aspirations unknowingly shape our future endeavors. The concept of taking flight, whether metaphorically or literally, symbolizes our desire for freedom, growth, and reaching new heights. Just like a bird that leaves its nest to explore the vast skies, we too yearn to break free from comfort zones and embrace the unknown.

The journey towards leadership and mentorship requires a strong sense of focus. By honing in on our goals and aspirations, we can navigate challenges with resilience and determination. A clear vision not only guides our own path but also serves as a beacon for those we lead and mentor.

In reflecting on the significance of focus in these roles, we uncover the power of intentionality and direction. Leaders and mentors who channel their energy towards a specific purpose can inspire others to do the same. By nurturing a culture of focus and dedication, we create a ripple effect of growth and success that extends far beyond our immediate sphere of influence.

So, let us spread our wings of focus and soar towards our aspirations, just like the bird that once dreamt of leaving its nest. In doing so, we embrace the transformative journey of leadership and mentorship with purpose and passion.

Hand-Gliding Experience

My dream of flight found its realization when I took a hand-gliding course while residing in Europe. The scenario unfolds, I was determined to turn my childhood dreams into reality, embarking on this adventurous journey. The crucial lesson lies not just in the soaring heights I reached but in the meticulous focus, I applied during the hand-gliding course.

As I soared through the clear blue skies, feeling weightless and free, I couldn't help but be amazed at the beauty of the world below. The wind whispered through my hair, carrying me higher and higher with each passing moment.

With each twist and turn, I felt more connected to the air around me, understanding the subtle dance of lift and gravity that kept me afloat. The world looked different from up there - small, insignificant worries faded away, replaced by a sense of awe and wonder at the vastness of the world.

It was in those moments of pure exhilaration that I realized the true power of chasing dreams and pushing boundaries. The hand-gliding course was not just about learning to fly, but about discovering the strength and determination within myself to conquer new heights, both literally and metaphorically.

As I landed back on solid ground, a smile spread across my face, knowing that I had achieved something truly remarkable. The experience had changed me in ways I could never have imagined, leaving me with a newfound sense of confidence and a deep appreciation for the endless possibilities that life has to offer.

FOCUS: A Mentor's Perspective

Drawing from my background, let's delve into the acronym FOCUS and its significance from a mentor's viewpoint.

F - Follow Essential Instructions: In the hand-gliding scenario, safety hinged on my ability to follow the essential instructions provided by my instructors. A mentor emphasizes the importance of adherence to guidelines, as success often lies in meticulous execution.

O - Overcome Distractions: Distractions can divert one from the path to success. My journey teaches others that maintaining focus requires overcoming external distractions and staying committed to the task at hand.

C - Cultivate Resilience: Challenges are inevitable, but cultivating resilience ensures that setbacks do not derail the journey. A mentor encourages mentees to view challenges as opportunities for growth and to persevere in the face of adversity.

U - Utilize Feedback: My progress in hand-gliding was facilitated by my openness to feedback. A mentor stresses the importance of utilizing constructive criticism to refine skills and continuously improve.

S - Set Clear Goals: My childhood dream acted as a compass, guiding me toward a specific goal. A mentor encourages individuals to set clear, achievable objectives, providing direction and purpose to their endeavors.

Scenario: The Importance of FOCUS in Hand-Gliding

Imagine being suspended in the air, hand-gliding against the backdrop of a breathtaking European landscape. In this scenario, you encounter unexpected turbulence. The wind challenges your control, and distractions vie for your attention. Your focus becomes your lifeline as you follow essential instructions, overcome distractions, cultivate resilience, utilize feedback, and stay committed to your goal of a safe descent.

Zig Ziglar said, "You don't have to be great to start, but you have to start to be great." This quote resonates with my journey, highlighting the importance of taking the first step and staying focused on the path ahead.

Roy T. Bennett said, "Focus on your strengths, not your weaknesses. Focus on your character, not your reputation." I feel Bennett's words exemplify the power of focusing on strengths and character, propelling you to achieve what seemed like unattainable dreams.

Questions and Answers:

Q: How did my childhood dream influence my adult life?
A: My childhood dream served as a driving force, inspiring me to take risks and pursue unconventional paths, culminating in my hand-gliding adventure.

Q: What role did focus play in my hand-gliding experience?
A: Focus was pivotal in the hand-gliding journey, ensuring that I followed instructions, overcame distractions, and stayed committed to achieving my goal.

Q: How can mentors instill the value of focus in their mentees?
A: Mentors can share stories, emphasizing the importance of focus, guiding setting clear goals, and encouraging resilience in the face of challenges.

Summary

My childhood dreams and hand-gliding adventures illuminate the transformative power of focus in leadership and mentorship. The FOCUS acronym, inspired by those life-changing experiences, serves as a guide for mentors to impart essential lessons, emphasizing the significance of following instructions, overcoming distractions, cultivating resilience, utilizing feedback, and setting clear goals.

Conclusion

In the tapestry of leadership and mentorship, My story stands as a demonstration to the profound impact of FOCUS. As mentors, we have the privilege of guiding others on their journeys, instilling in them the importance of staying focused amid challenges. By weaving the lessons from Betty's life into our mentorship approach, we empower individuals to navigate uncharted territories with resilience, purpose, and unwavering focus.

DR. BETTY SPEAKS

About Dr. Betty Speaks: Dr. Speaks is a United States Army retiree, the CEO of A Life Change NOW, and Podcast Host of Overcoming Battles by Being Strong and Courageous. The Artist/ Songwriter of the Single "It's A Resurrection. She is your Lifetime IMPRINT EMPRESS! She is very passionate about MOTIVATING individuals to resurrect and establish themselves spiritually, personally, or professionally. She's that chosen warrior who inspires others to create A Life Change Now by leaving an INTENTIONAL IMPACTFUL IMPRINT for INFINITY.

Betty is extremely passionate about helping individuals establish themselves and their generational wealth via multiple streams of income plus securing their retirement endeavors.

She also mentors youthful ladies and other individuals or teams during Transformational Workshops or One-On-One Mentorship, and other Total Well-Being Events. Betty Speaks… "IT" When She Speaks.

Author's Website: *www.BettySpeaks.com*

Book Series Website: *www.TheBookOfMentors.com*

"SET A GOAL TO ACHIEVE SOMETHING THAT IS SO BIG, SO EXHILARATING THAT IT EXCITES YOU AND SCARES YOU AT THE SAME TIME."

~ BOB PROCTOR

BOPI VILLARINO

BUILDING BRIDGES TO MASTERY

The Inspirational Pathway from Bob Proctor

In my journey through personal development and mentorship, I have had the privilege to learn from legends like Brian Tracy, whose teachings sharpened my understanding of real estate and enriched my personal life. As I ventured further, another monumental figure emerged as a cornerstone of my growth—Bob Proctor. His philosophy around the "science of getting rich" and personal mastery has influenced my career and my approach to life.

Continuing on my path of self-improvement, I delved into Bob Proctor's teachings with enthusiasm and curiosity. His profound insights on the power of the mind, the importance of setting clear goals, and the significance of consistent action resonated deeply with me. Through his guidance, I honed my strategic thinking in business and nurtured a mindset of abundance and positivity in all areas of my life.

Bob Proctor's emphasis on the "science of getting rich" revolutionized my financial strategies and transformed my mindset from scarcity to abundance. His focus on personal mastery encouraged me to strive for excellence in everything I do, reminding me that success is not just about external achievements but also inner growth and fulfillment.

As I continue integrating these invaluable lessons into my daily routine, I am grateful for the wisdom shared by mentors like Bob Proctor. Their influence has propelled my professional success, enriched my relationships, deepened my sense of purpose, and ignited a lifelong passion for continual growth and development. I am truly fortunate to have crossed paths with such remarkable individuals on my journey of self-discovery and empowerment.

My Encounter with Bob Proctor's Teachings

Bob Proctor's philosophy first intersected with my life during a period of transformation. After establishing a solid foundation in the real estate market and mentoring under the guidance of Brian Tracy, I felt a yearning for more profound knowledge—something that could transcend the typical boundaries of business success. Bob's teachings, which focus on the vibrational frequencies of success and the power of the mind, were a revelation. His ideas were not just strategies but a call to elevate one's entire being.

I fervently delved into Bob Proctor'sProctor's materials, immersing myself in his books, online courses, and seminars. His insights resonated profoundly, challenging me to shift my perspective and embrace a more expansive view of what was possible. As I applied his principles to my daily life, I noticed a significant transformation taking place within me. The concept of harnessing the power of my thoughts and beliefs to manifest my desires became a guiding principle, shaping my actions and decisions in a way that aligned with my deepest aspirations.

Bob Proctor's philosophy helped me succeed tremendously in my professional endeavors and fostered a sense of harmony and fulfillment in all aspects of my life. His emphasis on personal growth, positive energy, and unwavering faith in one's potential was a beacon of light during moments of doubt and uncertainty. Through his teachings, I learned to cultivate a mindset of abundance, gratitude, and resilience, paving the way for a journey of self-discovery and empowerment.

Today, I continue to draw inspiration from Bob Proctor's wisdom, integrating his teachings into my daily routine as I strive to reach new heights of achievement and fulfillment. His impact on my life has been nothing short of transformative, instilling in me a belief in the limitless possibilities that await those who dare to dream and take action. Bob

Proctor's philosophy remains a guiding force, reminding me that success is not just a destination but a lifelong journey of growth, discovery, and self-mastery.

Integrating Proctor's Principles

Bob's method of integrating the law of attraction with hardcore business tactics resonated deeply with me. He taught that success is not just about what you do but what you attract by the person you become. In real estate, this philosophy transformed how I approached negotiations, client relationships, and team management. Viewing my interactions through the lens of energy and attraction shifted my outcomes significantly, bringing more aligned and fruitful engagements.

Bob's teachings opened my eyes to a new perspective on achieving success. By blending the principles of the law of attraction with practical business strategies, I discovered the power of creating a positive energy within myself that extended to every aspect of my professional life. This mindset shift revolutionized how I conducted negotiations, built relationships with clients, and led my team. Instead of solely focusing on external actions, I prioritized personal growth and authenticity, knowing that the energy I put into the world would attract corresponding opportunities and connections. Embracing this holistic approach improved my outcomes and brought a sense of fulfillment and harmony to my business endeavors.

Expanding My Influence

Inspired by Bob Proctor, I expanded my role as a mentor. I began hosting workshops and seminars that focused on the mechanics of real estate and personal development and growth. As Bob had taught, I shared the importance of mindset, affirmations, and visualizations alongside practical business strategies with my mentees. This holistic approach was met with enthusiasm and success, reinforcing the profound impact of mentorship on personal and professional levels.

I witnessed firsthand how the fusion of real estate knowledge with personal development principles transformed my mentees. The workshops became a safe space for individuals to learn about property investment and delve into self-discovery and mindset shifts. Seeing them embrace affirmations to overcome self-limiting beliefs and use visualizations to manifest their goals with clarity and purpose was heartening.

As the workshops unfolded, a sense of empowerment and motivation filled the room, creating a ripple effect of positivity and growth. The success stories that emerged from these sessions served as a testament to the power of mentorship in nurturing professional success and personal fulfillment.

Through Bob Proctor's teachings and my own experiences, I learned that mentorship goes beyond imparting knowledge; it involves guiding and inspiring individuals to unlock their full potential. It was a journey of mutual learning and growth, during which I shared my expertise and gained valuable insights from each mentee's unique journey.

In mentorship, I discovered that the most profound transformations happen when we blend practical strategies with a deep focus on personal development. It was a rewarding experience to witness individuals excel in their real estate endeavors and evolve into empowered, self-assured individuals capable of achieving their dreams.

Challenging Conventional Success Metrics

Bob Proctor's teachings also challenged me to redefine success. Success was no longer about the number of sales or the business size but about the quality of life and the joy derived from everyday activities. This redefinition enhanced my well-being and helped me guide my mentees toward more sustainable and satisfying career paths.

Bob Proctor's teachings encouraged me to shift my perspective on success from external achievements to internal fulfillment. I began to understand that true success lies in finding joy in life's simple moments and maintaining balance and contentment. As I internalized this new definition of success, I found myself more at peace and content with where I was on my journey. This shift benefited me personally and allowed me to mentor others, focusing on holistic growth and long-term satisfaction in their careers. It's incredible how a simple change in mindset can lead to profound transformations in our personal and professional lives.

Mentoring with Compassion & Integrity

As I've learned from Brian Tracy and Bob Proctor, mentorship should be infused with compassion and integrity. I aimed to emulate these qualities, ensuring every interaction was rooted in genuine care and a deep desire to see others succeed. This approach has built long-lasting relationships that extend beyond mere business connections.

It's crucial to embody the essence of mentorship with a compassionate heart and unwavering integrity. Drawing inspiration from renowned figures like Brian Tracy and Bob Proctor, I have come to understand that the true essence of mentorship lies in genuine care and a sincere wish for the success of others. Through these values, I have cultivated relationships that transcend business transactions, fostering deep and lasting connections that enrich both parties.

Leveraging Personal Stories

One of the most potent tools I adopted from Bob Proctor's strategies was using personal stories to illustrate lessons. Sharing my journey, challenges, and how I overcame them made the lessons relatable and inspiring. This technique engaged my audience and encouraged them to share their stories, creating a rich tapestry of experiences within our workshops.

Utilizing personal anecdotes to convey lessons has proven to be a profound technique in my communication arsenal, inspired by Bob Proctor's wisdom. By recounting my trials, triumphs, and subsequent growth, I managed to weave a narrative that resonated deeply with my audience. This approach captivated the listeners and fostered an environment where they felt compelled yet comfortable enough to open up and share their narratives. Our workshops' collective sharing of stories has formed a vibrant mosaic of diverse experiences, enriching our sessions with authenticity and connection.

Continuous Learning & Adaptation:

Bob Proctor was a proponent of lifelong learning, a value I hold dearly. Staying updated and adaptable has been crucial in the ever-evolving real estate and personal development landscape. I continually seek new knowledge for my personal growth and enrich the mentoring I provide, keeping it relevant and impactful.

As my chapter in the legacy of mentorship continues to unfold, Bob Proctor's teachings remain a guiding light. His principles have shaped my professional landscape and enriched my personal life, allowing me to live with greater purpose and joy. Mentorship is a powerful journey that transforms, enhances, and transcends the ordinary, paving the way for a life of exceptional achievements and profound fulfillment.

BOPI VILLARINO

About Bopi Villarino: Raised in the picturesque La Costa Carlsbad, California, Bopi, has always been driven by a passion for education and real estate. She holds a Bachelor of Arts Degree in Liberal Studies/Elementary Education from Point Loma Nazarene University. As a dedicated mother to her beloved son Ross Villarino and cherished daughter-in-law Chelsea, Bopi takes pride in her role as a family-oriented individual. Bopi's remarkable journey into the world of real estate commenced at the young age of 18 when she served as a real estate assistant to a top-producing agent. She then ventured into the financial sector, establishing a mortgage company and expanding into the realms of real estate and escrow services.

After 15 years, Bopi successfully sold their business to a prominent nationwide brand. Bopi continued to soar in her career, assuming pivotal roles such as Vice President of the Western Region for a division of Lending Tree and Managing Partner for a substantial team in the bustling city of Los Angeles. Her versatile skill set encompasses positions such as manager, director of sales, and team lead across various real estate companies, spanning Southern California, Vail, Colorado, and Park City, Utah. Bopi became a certified real estate coach, extending her expertise to business owners and agents throughout the nation. Bopi took the courageous step of resigning from her role as the Utah Principal State Broker, where she oversaw a thriving community of 600+ agents. She founded Distinctive Properties, a real estate company nestled in the scenic beauty of Heber City, Utah. She finds solace and fulfillment in being in nature, and in various activities, including waterskiing, skiing/snowboarding, hiking, SUPing, snowshoeing, and camping.

Author's Website: *www.DistinctivePropertiesUtah.com*

Book Series Website: *www.TheBookOfMentors.com*

DANIEL KILBURN

WHAT DO YOU WANT?

Bob Proctor is a name well-known within the self-development industry. Born in the early 1930s, he was a youngster when Napoleon Hill's *Think and Grow Rich* was published. Though his education was limited, his appetite for knowledge and self-improvement did eventually lead him to the book *Think and Grow Rich*, marking the beginning of his journey to understanding the human mind and its potential.

Bob Proctor's path was not straightforward. He was a human, after all, and faced many challenges, setbacks, and failures. Once he started working with personal development giants like Earle Nightingale and Lloyd Conant, his breakthrough was astounding.

As their mentee, Proctor's personal growth developed, and he soon became a well-known speaker, author, and coach. He teaches a blend of historical wisdom, wrapped in modern science, focusing on the empowerment of an individual's ability to harness their full potential.

Influence on the Personal Development Industry

Bob Proctor's influence on the personal development industry is monumental. He is considered one of the most influential experts on mindset and success.

For over fifty years, he has taught millions through his books, seminars, and personal coaching. His work has helped individuals achieve personal and financial success and elevated the entire industry. Proctor's approach to personal development is holistic and comprehensive, addressing the

101

mental, emotional, and spiritual aspects of growth. He emphasizes the importance of mindset, beliefs, and the power of thoughts in shaping one's reality.

One of Proctor's significant contributions is his simplifying complex concepts and making them accessible. He has a unique talent for breaking down the laws of the universe and the principles of success into actionable steps anyone can follow. Proctor's teachings have bridged the gap between the mystical and the practical with everyday applications of his principles.

Overview of Core Concepts

Bob Proctor believes that we have the power to shape our lives through our thoughts, emotions, and actions. His core concepts are now fundamental in the personal development industry. He was ahead of the times.

At the core of Proctor's teachings is the idea that we are who we think we are. Therefore, if we do not like who we are, we need to change our minds.

The most powerful tool we have is our mind. In order to manifest our reality by changing our thinking patterns, we can change our lives. This concept is heavily influenced by the Law of Attraction, which suggests that like attracts like, and by focusing our thoughts on what we desire, we can bring it into our lives. It is extremely interesting that Bob Proctor describes the process of accomplishing our dreams, where others merely state it can be done.

Much has been noted in the last few years about an individual's vibrational energy. Proctor often discusses the importance of harmony with the universe and its immutable laws. Bob teaches that everything in the universe, including our thoughts, feelings, rocks, and trees have a specific vibration, and by aligning our personal vibration with what we want to achieve, we can attract those things into our lives.

Tell Me, What Do You Want?

Proctor often discusses the immense power of the subconscious mind. He believes that our subconscious beliefs shape our reality and that by reprogramming these beliefs, we can overcome limitations and achieve our goals. He provides strategies for accessing and influencing the subconscious to instill new, empowering beliefs.

Setting & Achieving Goals

Proctor outlines a detailed process for setting and achieving goals beyond wishful thinking. He emphasizes clarity, commitment, and understanding the 'why' behind your goals. His techniques involve visualizing the end result, acting as if the goal is already achieved, and taking consistent, purposeful action. Not the same as faking it till you make it, but being who you want to be. Who do you want to be?

Paradigm Shift

A significant focus of Proctor's work is on shifting paradigms and the mental programs that govern our behavior and outcomes. Many people operate within limiting paradigms and, by changing these, we can dramatically change our results. Proctor provides practical steps for identifying and altering these deep-seated beliefs.

One key actionable principle Bob Proctor describes is writing things down. As I write this chapter, 2023 is coming to an end. And the unfulfilled wonder and largess of 2024 stands before me.

Earlier this year, I came across a "Be, Have, Do" folder on a drive from an old computer. I flashed back in time, about twenty-plus years, and remember writing 100 things I wanted to Be, 100 things I wanted to Have, and 100 things I wanted to Do. After several minutes of checking things off, I realized I had accomplished 60% of the items in the three lists. What would have been the outcome if I had taken it seriously and focused on what I wanted?

While Bob is not the originator of the concept of the Law of Attraction, he is known for popularizing it. He teaches how to deliberately attract what you want by focusing on positive thoughts and feelings and by taking inspired action. He demystifies the process, making it accessible and practical for everyday use.

Creating a Positive Mental Attitude

A positive mental attitude is at the core of Proctor's teachings. He believes that optimism and a positive outlook are critical for success and happiness. Proctor often speaks about the importance of gratitude and focusing on what one already has rather than what one lacks. This shift in focus elevates one's mood and outlook and aligns them with the frequencies of abundance and success. What we focus on expands. Do we focus on lack and wonder why we have nothing, or are we grateful for what we have, drawing more of it to us?

Proctor teaches that emotions like fear, doubt, and worry are not just detrimental to one's happiness but also to one's ability to attract and manifest what one desires. He provides strategies to combat these negative emotions, such as replacing fear with curiosity, doubt with belief, and worry with action.

Moreover, Proctor encourages individuals to take responsibility for their mental state and not become a victim to external circumstances. He promotes an attitude of resilience and empowerment, where obstacles become opportunities for growth and learning.

The Process of Setting & Achieving Goals

Bob Proctor has revolutionized the process of setting and achieving goals with his unique and self-driven approach. He emphasizes that goal setting is not just about wishing for something; it's about clearly defining what you want, understanding why, and taking action to create it. In other words, you really need to think about what you want, why you want it, and what this desire will do for you, those you love, and the world. Unfortunately, many people cannot complete this process because they have not been taught how to think. Only to react.

Proctor insists that goals should be big and audacious, not limited by current circumstances or past experiences. He often quotes Napoleon Hill, saying, "What the mind can conceive and believe, it can achieve."

During the remainder of 2023, I am willing and grateful for writing down on paper "what do I want" in 2024. Since I am the creator of my reality, I am 100% responsible for the outcomes I create.

As we continue to explore Proctor's teachings, the importance of goal setting and continuous education as a tool for personal growth becomes increasingly apparent. Set your goals high and listen not to those with no desire or the will to accomplish greatness in their lives.

Practical Applications in Daily Life

Get ready to transform your life with the power of affirmations! Proctor knows just how crucial it is to speak positive, present-tense statements that reflect the achievement of your goals. But it doesn't stop there: He suggests recording and listening to these affirmations with heartfelt emotion and unwavering belief. After all, whose voice do you trust the most?

But that's not all. Proctor also urges you to embrace an attitude of gratitude. By focusing on and appreciating what you already have, you'll operate from a state of abundance, attracting even more good things into your life.

And remember, action is key. While Proctor highlights the importance of thought and belief, he reminds us that they must be followed by action. He encourages inspired actions that align with your goals, as they are the tangible results of your thoughts and beliefs.

Take a tip from Proctor's book, *Change Your Paradigm, Change Your Life*, and try a powerful morning exercise. Start your day by writing down ten things you're grateful for. You'll set a positive tone for the entire day. So, what are you grateful for?

Continuing Influence After Proctor

While Bob Proctor is no longer with us, his teachings will live on. The numerous coaches, speakers, and authors he has influenced will continue to spread his message, each adding their own insights and experiences.

The community that has formed around Proctor's teachings is a testament to their effectiveness and impact. Individuals from all over the world share their success stories and support each other in applying these principles, ensuring that his legacy will endure.

In conclusion, Bob Proctor's influence on personal development is both significant and lasting.

His teachings have provided a foundation for countless individuals to transform their lives, and his principles continue to inspire and guide new generations. As we look to the future, it's clear that the insights and strategies Proctor shared will remain an influential part of the personal development landscape, continuing to empower people to unlock their full potential and achieve their greatest dreams.

Tell me, what do you want?

DANIEL KILBURN

About Daniel Kilburn: Daniel Kilburn, America's 5-Star Leadership Coach is an urban disaster and financial planning expert with over 30 years of experience training foreign nationals, and Department of Defense Civilians to survive on the modern battlefield. He is the author of "Family Urban Disaster Planning" and co-author of the number one best-seller *The Book of Influence & The Book of Mentors*. Daniel has been featured in WFLA News Channel 8, Authority Magazine, and Lifestyles over 50.

Daniel helps parents open communications, build leadership, and develop resiliency to leave a legacy for their children.

Contact Daniel to discover the Finance and Family Protection Method at: *www.eapdan.com.*

Author's Website: *www.DanielKilburn.com*

Book Series Website: *www.TheBookOfMentors.com*

DAWNESE OPENSHAW

DREAM, DARE, DO: THE POWER OF MENTORSHIP

Mentorship is a journey of a transformative experience that can utterly reshape our beliefs, actions, and, ultimately, our lives.

At the heart of this transformational journey lies a mentor, a guiding force, who not only imparts knowledge but ignites a spark within us to dream bigger, dare greatly, and do the extraordinary. In the realm of mentorship, few names resonate as profoundly as Bob Proctor, whose influence and teachings have empowered countless individuals to choose to dream big, embrace faith over fear, live a life by design instead of by default, and achieve remarkable success personally and professionally.

At its core, mentorship embodies a symbiotic relationship where wisdom, inspiration, and guidance flow from mentor to mentee. And is a mutually beneficial to mentor and mentee. The guidance of a mentor is about having someone by your side who can inspire and motivate you to go beyond your comfort zone and beyond what you thought was ever possible.

Bob is one of those mentors who embodied the transformative power of mentorship. He didn't just inspire; he was a catalyst for change in individuals ready to break out of their box and go beyond the status quo —people who were and are ready to dream, dare, and do the extraordinary. His vision and his work of transformation continue with his team today and with all of the people he impacted through his mentoring.

Though I did not have the opportunity to meet Bob Proctor in person or to be mentored by him directly, I have had the opportunity learn so much from him through many videos and a lot of incredibly valuable program material. I've been greatly impacted by him, his vision, philosophies, and who he was in this world.

I have also had the opportunity to be mentored by people who were directly mentored by Bob. Some of these amazing mentors worked side by side with him at the Proctor Gallagher Institute and they were every bit powerful representatives of him and his mentorship. In fact, it was in 2016 when I was first introduced to Bob (beyond what I saw in "The Secret") through one of his mentors and I was instantly hooked.

It was through this very first program of Bob's that I participated in, with the support of my mentor, that I created my big goal—my Vision, my DREAM—that I'm living out right now.

Central to Bob Proctor's mentoring is the concept of setting audacious goals. The program I did was no exception. He said, "Set a goal to achieve something that is so big, so exhilarating that it excites you and scares you at the same time." I like to say create a goal so big that you feel like you want to throw up, but you don't.

These big audacious goals aren't about just any ordinary ambition; they are about aligning your goals with your spiritual core, crafting a vision that resonates deeply in your soul and propels you forward with an unwavering passion. Bob encourages us to seek goals that evoke chills, signifying their profound significance in our life journey. This is exactly what I did.

In this Proctor Gallagher program I participated in, I was encouraged to set my big audacious goal—my moon shot—which I wrote on a goal card and was invited to carry in my wallet so it was always close.

Well, I have carried this goal card in my wallet for eight years and I can now say it's finally coming to fruition. What does it say on my goal card? Well, I'm so glad you asked. It states, "I am so happy and grateful now that…."

I look and feel great in my NEW size 16 wardrobe. I've got an abundance of purposeful and positive energy as the Director of a Global Leadership Academy. We are developing the next generation of mindful (purpose-driven) leaders worldwide through the generous donations of local and global supporters, totaling $1,000,000.

In September of 2023, I opened the doors to the Global Leadership Academy with our first program being the Teen Leadership Experience. It was spectacular and is continuing to grow and expand as we add parents of teens into the conversation and opportunities for them to be mentored as well.

We are adding new trainings, one of which is a training for corporations and small businesses to send their emerging leaders (young adult leaders) to be coached and mentored in their creating responsibility and self-leadership. This generation now entering the workforce is passionate about making a difference and being impactful. What better way for them to learn how to create responsible and lasting impact than with a seasoned mentor by their side?!

I'm still working on the size 16 wardrobe and the $1,000,000 and I'm confident both will certainly be created.

As I have personally learned, the impact of mentorship goes even beyond setting goals and beyond external achievements; it delves into the realm of an inner transformation. It was in this program a significant internal transformation began for me. Bob himself emphasized, "Your outside world is a reflection of your inside world. What goes on in the inside shows on the outside." This shows me how important it is to create inner alignment—alignment in heart, body, mind, and spirit—to create personal growth resulting in achieving external success.

In the face of whatever challenges and adversity we experience in life as we move toward the creation of our audacious goal or dream, Bob's wisdom speaks to a sense of empowerment. He reminded us, "There is no problem outside of you that is superior to the power within you." All of the answers we need to create our goals and DREAMS are within us already. A mentor is someone who helps bring them to the surface and encourages us to DARE and to take action—to DO.

When we face challenges, a mentor can redirect our focus from the external obstacles to shift into our internal strength and resourcefulness. A mentor's role is not to shield us from challenges but to empower us to confront them with courage and confidence, knowing that our greatest assets lie within.

Bob Proctor's mentoring philosophy extends beyond individual growth to encompass life's overarching design. He asserts, "Life either happens by design or default. You choose." The power is within us to choose how we want to live, love, and lead. The power is within us to choose to DREAM, to be DARING, and to DO what brings joy into our lives and the lives of others. The power to choose is as significant as life itself and having a mentor to guide you along this path is a blessing.

The conscious decision to design our lives with intention, purpose, and clarity. With a mentor like Bob, individuals embark on a journey of self-discovery, aligning our actions with our aspirations and creating a life that reflects our deepest desires. It's about unlocking our potential, challenging limitations, and embracing the full spectrum of possibilities available to us.

Mentorship isn't just about acquiring knowledge or skills; it's about undergoing a profound shift in consciousness, and is a journey of self-discovery, especially under the guidance of a powerful mentor. Mentorship is about unlocking our potential, challenging our limitations, and embracing the full spectrum of possibilities. This partnership between mentor and mentee transcends boundaries, leading to profound transformations that ripples through every aspect of life.

As Bob puts it, "If you want something that's beyond your reach, dream, dare, and do with a mentor. And if you want something extraordinary—something you have no idea how to do—dream, dare, and do with an extraordinary mentor."

Having a mentor is like having a personal a catalyst for change in your pocket. It's having someone in active partnership with you to create success in all the areas of your life. They are your own personal cheerleader and kick in the pants coach who won't let you sit down and put your head in your hands for long. A mentor can have significant influence in your life, should you choose one.

They will support and guide you toward having the faith to reach your audacious goals, create inner resilience, and be intentional in how you choose to design your extraordinary life.

The possibilities of what can be created with an extraordinary mentor, like a Bob, alongside you in your journey...well, they are endless. And these endless possibilities are available to you when you lean in, learn from others who have walked the talk, and will support you to DREAM your big dream—to have the courage to DARE to make it happen—and encourage you to DO whatever it takes to make your dream come true.

If you haven't already, NOW is the time to find an extraordinary mentor for you to create your extraordinary goals and to live the life of your dreams.

DAWNESE OPENSHAW

About Dawnese Openshaw: Dawnese Openshaw is an agent for CHANGE and is a radically authentic transformational leadership and relationship coach. She is also a John Maxwell certified leadership coach, trainer, and speaker in addition to being a published author in *The Principles of David and Goliath* book series and *The Book of Influence* series and has co-authored a book for adoptive moms.

With over 26 years of experience in small business and non-profit organizations, in 2020 Dawnese expanded her coaching to include families which is now her main focus. She teaches emotional intelligence, communication, and relationship building. She combines her passion for leadership and commitment with strengthening families, primarily serving families with teens. Dawnese empowers families to heal individually and together, creating love and harmony in their hearts and home.

She has been married to her husband, Scott, for 28 years and they are the parents of three amazing children (Randy - 25, Thaniel - 24, and Kayden - 19). They grew their family this summer when Randy got married, adding a beautiful daughter-in-law (Mo).

Author's Website: *www.FullyInvestedFamilies.com*

Book Series Website: www.TheBookOfMentors.com

DONNA MINER

MANIFESTATION EXPERIENCES & BELIEFS

"Act as if you have it now."
~ **Bob Proctor**

Visualization has played more of a significant role in my life than I realized. As I look back on my life, I can see many instances where I used visualization without necessarily even knowing it, as well as other times when I was very intentional. I emphasize the importance of preparation, authenticity, and empathy in personal interactions.

In one memorable instance, I helped my daughter harness the power of visualization to enhance her performance in competitive softball. She was initially skeptical, but I was determined to show her how impactful a clear, focused mind could be.

"Come stand by this tree," I instructed her. "Close your eyes and hold your bat in your hand." As she complied, I guided her through a vivid visualization. "Imagine the smell of the grass," I began, and she nodded, her eyes still closed. "Can you hear the noises around you?" I asked. "Yeah," she responded.

"Now, imagine you're at home plate," I continued. I described the opposing team's pitcher, whom I had seen before, to help her paint a clearer mental picture. "This is what she looks like, and this is how she pitches," I explained. I wanted her to feel the moment's reality, to believe in her presence at the plate. "Make eye contact with her, feel confident."

As I guided her, I narrated the unfolding scene: "Her arm is coming around, she's releasing the ball, and it's coming straight towards your bat." I urged my daughter to visualize hitting the ball at the perfect sweet spot. "The ball is soaring—do you see it?" I asked. Excitedly, she whispered, "Yes, I see it."

In the actual game, the result of this mental preparation was astounding. She hit a double, a significant achievement. "What?" she exclaimed afterward, unable to believe the outcome. Years have passed, and she barely remembers that day, but I recall it vividly. It was a profound demonstration of how visualization could bridge the gap between potential and performance, leaving a lasting impact on both of us. This experience reinforced my belief in the power of the mind and its crucial role in achieving personal success.

In my journey of self-discovery and growth, I have found that manifestation is not merely wishful thinking but a powerful tool that can shape our reality. By visualizing our goals with clarity and intention, we set a series of actions and events that align with our desires.

Reflecting on the milestones I have reached, I realize the profound impact of visualization. It is like painting a vivid picture in our minds and then working diligently to turn that vision into a tangible reality.

Furthermore, I have learned that preparation is critical to success. By trying to equip ourselves with the necessary skills and knowledge, we pave the way for our aspirations to materialize. Authenticity also plays a crucial role in manifestation. Being true to ourselves and our values allows us to attract opportunities that resonate with our genuine selves.

Lastly, empathy is a powerful force that fosters meaningful connections and collaborations. By approaching personal interactions with compassion and understanding, we not only enrich our own lives but also contribute positively to the lives of those around us.

In essence, manifestation is a dynamic process that involves clarity of vision, diligent preparation, authenticity, and empathy. By embracing these principles, we can unlock our full potential and create a life filled with purpose, fulfillment, and abundance.

Bob counseled us to talk to ourselves like we already had it: "You already have it. Bring it in."

Intentionality, Visualization, & Compound Effects

There is the power of intentionality and visualization in achieving one's goals. I emphasize the importance of being intentional about what I want and not just unquestioningly wanting things. Small, daily achievements can lead to significant results over time, a concept known as the compound effect. Here's a vivid example of how I once manifested something in my life, which at first seemed like a mere coincidence:

Years ago, during a challenging period as a single mom, I found solace in the little rituals of hope and visualization. One such ritual involved the old Calgon bath salts commercials, which depicted a woman escaping her troubles in a soothing bath. At night, I'd lie in bed and whisper, "Calgon, take me away," imagining myself in that serene, problem-free bath. It wasn't just a plea for escape; I was visualizing a different, more peaceful life.

Years before this, in college, my ex-husband and I were asked to house-sit for his aunt and uncle. Their home was my first encounter with luxury of such kind—they had a shower equipped with a squeegee, symbolizing the pinnacle of wealth. "One day, I'm going to have a squeegee," I thought, amused yet inspired by the thought.

Fast forward to 1997, amidst my divorce. Those commercial scenes and my wishes for tranquility resonated deeper. I longed for that bath, that escape, not expecting anything to come of it.

Then, in 2002, something incredible happened. My new husband and I were building a house, and due to a contractor's error, a large jetted tub was installed in our bathroom—an upgrade we hadn't asked for. They told us it was too costly to replace what we originally planned, so the tub stayed. It struck me profoundly when I realized—there I was, in my luxurious bath, the kind I had dreamed of during those hard times. I even had a squeegee in my shower, just like the one I envied in college.

It dawned on me then: had I manifested this? This realization came fully when, years later, a speaker asked if anyone had ever manifested something. Reflecting on my journey, I understood that those nights of hopeful visualization weren't just idle dreams—they were powerful intentions, crafting my reality in ways I hadn't fully understood until that tub was right before me.

Zig Ziglar and Bob Proctor used similar teachings together, and I reflect on how familiar Proctor's messages sounded because of this possible connection. A specific visualization practice that Bob Proctor promotes emphasizes the effectiveness of imagining oneself in the possession of one's desires as if one already has them.

This visualization technique encourages individuals to immerse themselves deeply in the experience of having already achieved their goals. By vividly picturing themselves living their dream life, feeling the emotions of success, and seeing the world through the lens of accomplishment, they can align their thoughts and actions with their aspirations. Bob Proctor's approach underscores the power of the mind in shaping one's reality, inspiring individuals to manifest their desires by first believing in their attainment. Through consistent practice and unwavering belief, this visualization method can be a powerful tool in realizing personal goals and fostering a mindset of abundance and achievement.

Embracing Natural Flow for Success

Bob Proctor often spoke about the natural flow of the universe and how aligning with it can lead to success. He taught me to embrace this flow and tap into the rhythm of life surrounding us. It's not just about going with the flow but actively creating your path by harmonizing with the universe's inherent movements.

Ignoring the naysayers and focusing on my path has been crucial. For instance, I've always been inspired by those who dared to dream big despite the odds. There's this individual I know who never let logic dictate his potential. He had a vision and relentlessly pursued it, not just dreaming but planning and executing against all odds. His success wasn't just by chance but a testimony to the power of steadfast belief in one's vision.

"People have the capacity to create anything they want in life, and success is largely a result of mindset rather than strategy."
~ Bob Proctor

Mindset's Role in Achieving Success

Bob Proctor said, "People have the capacity to create anything they want in life, and success is largely a result of mindset rather than strategy." This resonates deeply with me. It's about how you think, perceive, and respond to the world around you. By adopting a mindset geared towards growth and possibilities, I opened myself up to opportunities I might have otherwise overlooked. I surround myself with reminders of this mindset. These motivate me and reinforce the mindset that I can achieve anything I want.

Bob's Impact, Lessons, & Manifestation

Bob's teachings dramatically changed the way I viewed life and success. His lessons on the power of the subconscious mind and the law of attraction helped me to harness my inner potential. Stories like that of Jamie Kern Lima, who turned her rejection into a monumental success story through sheer belief and determination, reminds us all that setbacks can be set up for greater comebacks.

Jamie Kern Lima's journey is a powerful testament to the idea that setbacks can be set up for monumental comebacks. Her story is particularly resonant because it showcases personal resilience and the profound impact of maintaining a positive mindset and steadfast belief in one's vision despite daunting challenges.

Jamie started her career as a news anchor but soon realized a need in the beauty industry for more inclusive makeup. She co-founded IT Cosmetics because she struggled with her camera appearance due to her rosacea. Despite creating a product she believed in, Jamie faced immense rejection. One pivotal moment came when a potential investor told her that her product would fail because she was not conventionally attractive enough to represent a beauty brand. This rejection was profoundly personal and could have deterred a less determined soul.

However, Jamie interpreted this rejection as not a final verdict but a challenge to push harder. She held onto her belief that there was a place in the market for her products—a strong faith that seemed to manifest her destiny. She continued pitching her product relentlessly and finally got a breakthrough when IT Cosmetics was given a 10-minute airing slot on QVC. Jamie went live, demonstrated her product's effectiveness on herself, and sold out in under 10 minutes. This success on QVC was just the beginning. IT Cosmetics grew exponentially and was eventually acquired by L'Oréal for $1.2 billion, one of the largest sums ever paid for a beauty brand.

Jamie's story embodies the principles of visualization and manifestation that Bob Proctor teaches. She visualized her success, held onto her vision despite adversities, and took actionable steps aligned with her goals. Her journey underscores that a positive mindset, unwavering faith, and action can transform dreams into reality.

Personal Development Journeys & Visualization

One of my long-held dreams has been to coach clients while looking at the ocean. This vision is vivid in my mind—I can almost feel the breeze and hear the waves. It's not just a dream but a goal I'm actively working towards. The right frequency of thought attracts the right people into our lives, making our dreams achievable. The books I read, like *The Greatest Salesman in the World* by Og Mandino, reinforce these concepts and are part of my daily mental and professional diet.

Embracing Mindfulness & Simple Pleasures

I've learned to appreciate the simple moments, like quiet mornings when I can be still and reflect. My father taught me the value of being present. It's easy to rush through life without noticing the beauty, but slowing down enriches our life experience. I keep reminders, like the one on my phone, that prompt me to pause and be still, helping me connect more deeply with the present moment.

Gratitude & Mindfulness for a Better Life

Every morning, I make it a point to practice gratitude. Today, for instance, I was struck by the beauty of the dawn sky. Moments like these remind us of life's beauty, encouraging a positive start to the day. I share these moments to inspire others to find beauty in their daily lives, urging them to embrace stillness and mindfulness. This practice doesn't just enhance our days—it transforms our entire approach to life, grounding us in what truly matters.

Taking the time to appreciate the small wonders around us can profoundly impact our well-being and outlook. By cultivating gratitude and mindfulness, we open ourselves to a world of beauty and positivity that might have gone unnoticed. So, let us all strive to start each day with a grateful heart and a keen eye for the beauty surrounding us, for it is in these moments that we find true joy and fulfillment.

DONNA MINER

About Donna Miner: Donna Miner is a seasoned Account Representative with over 25 years of experience in the real estate industry. Since 1996, she has been a pivotal figure in the sector, showcasing her expertise in sales and her dedication to fostering long-lasting relationships. Donna's passion lies in being an integral part of others' success, taking immense pride in witnessing her clients' personal and professional growth. Her professional journey began at U.S. Title, where she served as a Licensed Escrow Officer in 1996. Donna then transitioned to First American Title Company, where she held dual roles as an Account Executive and Licensed Escrow Officer for over 12 years. Since 2012, Donna has been a Sales Executive at Old Republic Title, located in Clearfield, Utah.

Donna has been the recipient of several prestigious awards, including the Presidents Award by Old Republic Title Central Division in 2022 and the $1,000,000 Producer Award for 2021. Additionally, the Northern Wasatch Board of Realtors honored her with the Presidential Achievement Award in 2021. Earlier in her career, while associated with First American Title Company, she was recognized as the Member of the Year by the Northern Wasatch Women's Council of Realtors in 2011 as well as Affiliate of the Year presented by the Weber-North Davis Board of Realtors in 2004 and 2006. Beyond her professional achievements, Donna is actively involved with committees associated with the Northern Wasatch Board of Realtors as an affiliate and maintains her escrow license. Donna spent many years singing in a band and is now a Sales Representative for a national title company. Her journey has also led her to become a certified Sales Mindset Coach under Jay Shetty's guidance. Her true sanctuaries are found on her patio and the beach, and her most cherished bonds are with her family and close friends.

Book Series Website: *www.TheBookOfMentors.com*

"IF YOU SEE IT IN YOUR MIND, YOU WILL HOLD IT IN YOUR HAND."

~ BOB PROCTOR

EILEEN E. GALBRAITH

EMBRACE YOUR UNLIMITED POTENTIAL: A JOURNEY OF SELF-DISCOVERY

First, a brief story I think most of us can relate to—this is my introduction to myself, I hope you enjoy!

In the heart of a bustling city, where towering buildings cast long shadows and bustling streets echoed with the hurried footsteps of passersby, lived a timid young girl named Elizabeth. Elizabeth found herself lost in the maze of life's complexities, her heart heavy with the weight of uncertainty and fear. Yet, amidst the chaos, a glimmer of hope appeared in the form of a weathered book, *You Were Born Rich* by Bob Proctor.

Elizabeth's trembling hands reached out to grasp the book, its title promising a world beyond her wildest dreams. As she delved into its pages, she discovered a treasure trove of wisdom that would alter the course of her life forever. Bob Proctor's teachings on the power of the mind resonated deeply with Elizabeth, offering a glimpse of a reality where fear no longer held sway.

With each word she read, Elizabeth felt a shift within herself—a newfound sense of courage and determination began to blossom in her heart. The concept of goal setting emerged as a guiding light, illuminating a path through the darkness of her fears. No longer mere wishes, her goals became beacons of hope, leading her towards a future filled with promise and possibility.

Inspired by Proctor's teachings, Elizabeth embarked on a journey of self-discovery, armed with the tools of visualization and affirmation. In the quiet moments of the night, she closed her eyes and dared to dream of a life beyond her imagination. With each passing day, her visions grew clearer, her resolve stronger.

But it was consistent action that truly propelled Elizaberh forward on her journey. Despite her initial fears and doubts, she found the courage to take small steps towards her goals, trusting in the wisdom of Proctor's words. With each step, her confidence grew, until she stood tall in the face of adversity, ready to conquer whatever challenges lay ahead.

As Elizabeth's journey unfolded, she realized that the teachings of Bob Proctor were not just for her own benefit, but for the empowerment of others. She became a beacon of hope for fellow young women, inspiring them to pursue their dreams with clarity, confidence, courage, and conviction. Through her success in business, she paved the way for a new generation of female entrepreneurs, each one daring to defy the odds and claim their rightful place in the world.

And so, the timid young girl who once feared her own shadow blossomed into a confident and successful businesswoman, her story serving as a testament to the transformative power of Bob Proctor's teachings. In a world filled with uncertainty and doubt, Elizabeth's journey reminds us that with faith, determination, and the right mentor, anything is possible.

In a world filled with boundless possibilities, it's easy to lose sight of our own potential amidst the noise of everyday life. Yet, deep within each of us lies a reservoir of untapped potential waiting to be unleashed. It's time to embark on a journey of self-discovery, guided by the timeless wisdom of Bob Proctor, and unlock the greatness that resides within.

In my early adulthood, as I was embarking on my own journey of self-discovery, I came across a book called, *You Were Born Rich* by Bob Proctor, which came out the same year I was first married in 1984. I believe it was a gift from a friend. This book opened my eyes to amazing and wonderous possibilities. The principles outlined in *You Were Born Rich* offer a roadmap to a life filled with abundance, fulfillment, and purpose.

With clarity, confidence, and conviction, three of my favorite words and top principles I share with my personal clients, Proctor guides readers towards financial prosperity, personal growth, and spiritual enlightenment. Through practical exercises and timeless wisdom, individuals are empowered to awaken their innate potential and take control of their destiny. From that moment on, I was hooked on personal growth and developing my inner self-worth.

I strongly hold the belief that when a person is prepared to learn, the right mentor or teacher appears. This precise phenomenon unfolded for me when I delved into this book and absorbed its fundamental teachings. I found myself captivated by concepts that, while seemingly straightforward, felt out of reach. Thus, my journey commenced, and I've remained a dedicated student of personal development ever since.

As you embark on this life-changing journey, seize the opportunity to take action right now. I've distilled two key steps from Bob Proctor's transformative teachings to empower you along your path of personal growth. Let's dive into these two simple yet powerful actions that will propel you towards your own transformation.

Discovering Your Inner Beliefs

At the very core of who we are lie our beliefs and attitudes, silently shaping the world we perceive and the experiences we encounter. It's essential to take a moment to introspect and reflect on these innermost beliefs. Consider what you truly believe about yourself—your strengths, your abilities, your potential. Are there any beliefs that hold you back, whispering doubts and insecurities into your mind? Take a gentle yet honest look at these beliefs, approaching them with kindness and compassion.

Now, let's shift our focus to a pivotal question: What do you want? This question serves as a compass, guiding us towards our deepest desires and aspirations. Take a pen and paper, or open a blank document on your device, and jot down your immediate thoughts. Don't worry about crafting the perfect response; instead, let your intuition guide you. Write down whatever comes to mind, allowing your thoughts to flow freely.

It's worth noting that we often find ourselves fixating on what we don't want, inadvertently attracting more of the same into our lives. By consciously shifting our focus towards what we do want, we set into motion a powerful force of manifestation. So, as you contemplate this question, allow yourself to dream big. Visualize the life you desire—the career, the relationships, the experiences. Paint a vivid picture in your mind's eye, infusing it with passion and excitement.

Remember, this exercise is just the beginning of your journey towards transformation. By confronting your beliefs, clarifying your desires, and embracing the power of intention, you take the first step towards creating the life you truly deserve.

Harnessing the Power of Your Mind

Central to your journey of self-discovery is the understanding of the profound power of your mind. Your thoughts and beliefs act as the seeds that shape your reality. Practice the art of visualization and positive affirmations to reprogram your subconscious mind for success. Visualize yourself achieving your goals with vivid detail and affirm your inherent greatness with unwavering confidence.

In many of my programs, we include comprehensive exercises designed to help you fully concentrate on this aspect, unlocking boundless potential for personal and business advancement. This foundational process is essential for ensuring success on your journey.

As you navigate the twists and turns of your journey, embrace the process of growth and resilience. View challenges as opportunities for learning and development, knowing that each obstacle you overcome brings you one step closer to your dreams. Cultivate a mindset of resilience and perseverance, knowing that you can overcome any adversity that comes your way.

As you undergo your own transformation, remember the profound impact you have on those around you. Your journey serves as a beacon of hope and inspiration for others who may be seeking their own path to greatness. Share your wisdom, lend a helping hand, and inspire others to embrace their unlimited potential and embark on their own journey of self-discovery.

In conclusion, the journey of self-discovery is a transformative odyssey that leads us to the realization of our true potential. Guided by the timeless wisdom of Bob Proctor, we can unlock the greatness that resides within us and create lives of abundance, fulfillment, and purpose. Embrace your unlimited potential, set sail towards your dreams, and illuminate the path for others to follow.

The world is waiting for you to shine your light—are you ready to embark on the journey of a lifetime? Furthermore, I urge you to explore Bob Proctor's book, *You Were Born Rich*. It has profoundly enriched my life, and I am confident it will have a similar impact on yours.

EILEEN E. GALBRAITH

About Eileen E Galbraith: As a Financial Architect for Business, entrepreneurs hire Eileen to build their influence and scale their profits because most lack essential methods and channels to create success, lack funding opportunities, and may face continuous struggles resulting in business disarray. So, Eileen helps them define, align, and design a visible, credible, and sustaining business. Financial disarray is a precursor to failure—do not let that happen to your business!

Eileen is a Compassionate Kick-ass Coach. She can kick your butt in financial shape and make things happen, but she's also very compassionate. She knows what people need, what they want, and how to deliver it.

Eileen is a Certified FICO Pro, an International Best-Selling Author and Speaker, a sought-after Business Success Coach, and the Founder of Renewed Abundance and Credit Knowhow. She has run multi-million-dollar businesses throughout her career and increased cash flow and profitability throughout her markets. Recognized as a professional Business Coach, Eileen positions her clients toward optimal possibilities, such as optimizing their personal credit to position themselves to build credit in the name of their business. This all-important step opens the doors to Financial Creditability, Fundability, and Business Growth. Eileen has a high-energy, no-nonsense approach and loves supporting people with their goals. Just look for the Dancing Queen, and you will find Eileen!

For more information on credit, visit: *www.CreditKnowhow.biz*

Author's Website: *www.RenewedAbundance.com*

Book Series Website: *www.TheBookOfMentors.com*

ERIC D. JACKSON

NEGATIVE MENTORSHIP: WHEN SCIENCE BECOMES YOUR MENTOR

"The Law of Polarity - there is good and bad in everything.
Look for the good."
~ **Bob Proctor**

Calls to Action from Personal Values Toward Mentorship

Recently, I answered someone's question about how to help leaders with their observation skills.

The first thing a leader (mentor) needs to do, is increase their own self-awareness and self-management, as well as their relationship awareness and relationship management skills—AKA their EQ, or emotional intelligence. I'll share the second step later in this chapter—yes, wait… there's more!

Have you ever had a leader or a mentor who was more of a stumbling block to you and to others? It is highly probable we have all experienced poor leadership, or "Negative Mentorship." Most often, the mentor is probably unaware of their blind-spots (and bad habits). By definition, we cannot see all of our areas needing improvement. That person is likely an unconscious incompetent, and maybe there is hope for them yet. If there truly is no help for them to change—run, fast!

But that doesn't help you—yet, does it? It doesn't fix any negative mentorship experiences you have had in your life, other than recognizing, avoiding, and excusing yourself from future encounters. Hopefully.

> *"Let people know there's a better way. There's a light at the end of the tunnel. There's places to get help."*
> ~ Bob Proctor

That is why, for ourselves, and for those poor leaders or negative mentors, we need to realize that we all need good coaches. Good or even great coaches help us see our blind spots, so we can observe our own behaviors, see our own potential, overcome poor programming or faulty information, and influence better outcomes for ourselves and others. Then we can start fixing and overcoming some of those negative mentorship experiences.

Did you know there is actually a science as well as an art to growth and development? The scientific approach is exactly what Bob Proctor took when he was first introduced to Napoleon Hill's "Think and Grow Rich," and Nightingale-Cognant's content. He began his study and observation of the human mind, behavior, and potential as a daily practice that lasted his whole life.

And he wasn't shy about sharing how it fit his belief in God, the Natural Laws of the Universe, and the art of applying it all to transform your patterns and results in all areas of your life.

> *"Fatih moves us into a physical vibration called well-being."*
> ~ Bob Proctor

The main thing is to have a plan for lifelong growth and contribution. You can do it!

Bob Proctor said of himself that he went from being an unconscious incompetent to a conscious incompetent. He became aware of his limitations, and then he decided to do something about it. He set a goal to work for Nightingale-Cognant and became one of their senior executives, eventually starting his own institute for positive thinking and performance.

I have personally learned so much from Bob's work and I am still peeling layers of profound understanding that are helping me in my own journey. He laid the groundwork and influenced so many in the space of personal and professional growth and performance.

Bob Proctor sought after new mentors, new information, new behaviors, and a new mindset. At one stage of his early successes, he describes himself as an unconscious competent because he couldn't always explain why he was achieving certain successes, but at the peak of his career he was considered the "world's foremost expert on the mind."

The Proctor Gallagher Institute

His awareness and observation skills sure seem like they changed for the better. Wouldn't you agree? And yours can too when you also work on improving them in yourself. Bob Proctor ultimately went from being a kid with a poor self-image, little ambition, and no plans for his future all the way to achieving his wildest imaginations.

> *"It's not who you think you are that holds you back - it's who*
> *you think you're not."*
> ~ Bob Proctor

Bob dedicated his life to sharing what he learned with others. His legacy lives on in people like you and me who dedicate themselves to grow in the understanding and application of the timeless principles he shared with us. We can learn from Bob how our minds work, and how to design our paradigms, environments, and cultures to achieve greater results.

There are volumes of insights that wouldn't fit in all these chapters to honor Bob Proctor's work and influence. That just means you have some homework to do if you choose to!

Here are some values you can take into your mentorship opportunities that will serve you well:

- Accountability,
- Humility to Learn,
- Responsiveness, and
- Multiplication

Accountability: Bob quotes Emerson, that "the Law of Laws is Cause and Effect." This is why we have to be accountable to be Positive and not Negative Mentors, Leaders, and Coaches. There is a ripple effect to what we allow in our own lives, and what we influence, for better or worse, into someone else's life.

Humility: I like these quotes from Bob; "Willingly give. Graciously receive," and "Confidence is requisite to great understanding." It takes humility to show up as your whole self to contribute and be of greater service to others, as well as to graciously receive, and to display confidence with understanding.

Responsiveness: Bob says, "When you change the way you look at something, what you look at changes." Be willing to pause between a stimulus and your response so you can see things from different angles and perspectives. You still need to respond to the situations and environments or demands around you, and this will help you do it with more wisdom and insight.

Multiplication: Consider these thoughts from Bob when thinking about how your mentor is preparing you, or how you might prepare others to carry the torch on to the next generation of leaders: "The spirit is always for expansion and fuller expression," and "You don't get energy, you release it." What are you helping to expand? How can you allow a fuller expression of yourself, and of others? What energy is being released toward you? For you? What type of energy are you releasing toward or for others, and into each environment you enter?

> *"Life: Accept It, Harvest the Good, Forgive All the Rest."*
> ~ Bob Proctor

Oh yeah... I promised at the beginning to share the second step in improving observation skills in ourselves, and in other leaders, mentors, and coaches after first overcoming the negative mentorship experiences.

When we have purposed for ourselves to be more aware, then we can choose to see value, uniqueness, possibility, awe, and wonder all around us.

We can see all of that in the tiniest things around us, and across the vastness of space. We can see it all in the simplest systems and processes, as well as the most complex procedures and even chaotic whirlwinds.

Becoming an observer is becoming a scientist and an artist, both creative and analytical. As our abilities to observe the world around us increase we just might see it through the eyes and heart of a child and explore everything with joy and amazement.

Go create opportunities for yourself and others to boldly and confidently know it's okay to see the possibilities all around us. Invite others along for the journeys we can adventure on together!

Or, as Bob would answer, "The three skills you need are to be creative, allowing the free-flow of energy; be interested in new ideas; and ask yourself, how can I be of greater service?"

ERIC D. JACKSON

About Eric D. Jackson: Eric D Jackson is dedicated to aiding business leaders in achieving the transformations they desire in life, work, and finances. As a speaker, coach, and trainer affiliated with the Maxwell Leadership Team and SCALE Architects of Predictable Success, Jackson showcases his expertise in leadership and finance. Additionally, he manages his own insurance and financial services practice and is eagerly anticipating the release of three book projects.

In his role as a Financial and Leadership Coach, Jackson assists leaders in expanding their influence, strengthening their teams, and amplifying their impact. His core philosophy revolves around helping these leaders GAIN, RETAIN, and TRAIN the elements crucial to their success journey. As a strong advocate for personal growth, leadership, and culture development, Jackson wears many hats: author, content creator, and champion of #FFF - Faith, Family, and Freedom. He is a certified Coach, Trainer, and Speaker with Maxwell Leadership, a licensed SCALE Architect by Predictable Success, and a Licensed Financial Services Partner with certifications as CLU and MLO.

Jackson is the principal and recruiter for Leadership Life Finances LLC, offering commercial benefit solutions for business leaders through "Its YourLIF," catering to their insurance, financial, and training needs. He also serves as the Principal at Transformational Leadership & Culture Intn't LLC. One of his most significant passions lies in positively impacting individuals' lives, wherein he uplifts, motivates, and equips them for personal growth and success.

Jackson is also an established publisher, known for his journal/planner and success series, Forward & Upward. He's an author for the Mentorship Series and is collaborating on four volumes slated for release between Fall 2023 and Fall 2024. He's currently penning his first full-length nonfiction self-help book, designed to offer readers a unique tool to visualize and quantify their growth and success journey. This tool aims to help individuals make informed decisions promptly, understand their goals, implement new content more efficiently, and achieve the outcomes they deem most vital.

Author's Website: *ItsYourLif.com/links*

Book Series Website: *www.TheBookOfMentors*

ERIN LEY

THE INSIGHT TO LIVE YOUR BEST LIFE

Bob Proctor, author of the book, *You Were Born Rich*, brilliantly states, "See yourself where you want to be and then be there. Don't be in the past. Be there! Act like the person you want to become."

When Bob was struggling financially in his twenties with an income of $4,000 and $6,000 in debt, he met Ray Stanford, who went on to become his mentor. This gentleman handed Bob the book Think and Grow Rich by Napolean Hill and taught Bob about the Stickperson.

The Stickperson was his mentor's way of explaining what the conscious and subconscious mind are and their relationship with the body. The body is the instrument of the mind. Ray drew a circle with a line horizontally through the middle of it, illustrating the conscious mind on top and the subconscious mind on the bottom with five lines coming out of the top of the conscious mind, illustrating the five senses. The body was a stick figure below the circle. This stickperson transformed Bob's life in the most profound way.

Bob had taught this for over sixty years. The conscious mind takes in, through the senses, tons of stimulation and one of the most important jobs the conscious mind has is to filter in what is most important to us as individuals. What we focus on most is what gets deposited into the subconscious mind. The subconscious mind cannot reject anything, and it cannot determine if something is good or bad for us. It must accept it.

From birth to approximately eight years of age, we are an open funnel streaming into our subconscious mind the beliefs of others. Very little is conscious. We conform and capitulate so much of who we truly are to meet the needs of family and society. We take what they say as "truth" and it gets deposited into our subconscious mind where we then live out those "truths" for a lifetime.

The richness we are born with dissipates and it turns into a feeling of lack. Some go on to feel as though they are not good enough, others feel unworthy, and many others struggle with self-doubt, all because they took on the self-limiting beliefs of others. They are not conscious of this. However, once they become aware of what Bob refers to as the paradigm, a cluster of habits and beliefs stored in the subconscious mind, we can release what is not serving us and replace those habits and beliefs with ones that will serve us.

Another one of Bob's books is *Change Your Paradigm Change Your Life*, where he explains that the paradigm will not go away without a fight. It wants to stay exactly where it is, keeping you from living your best life. The only way we can break down the paradigm is through:

1. An emotional impact, usually something negative. This is an undesirable experience and disempowering.

2. Elite level coaching. This is the preferred method and is extremely empowering with proper support.

The paradigm dies of neglect as you focus on the beliefs and habits that will grow your life, reuniting yourself with the richness of life you were born with.

Bob was very good when speaking with someone who started making excuses for not being able to do what they wanted to do. He would say, "I'm laughing, not at you, but because I know I'm no longer speaking with you. I'm speaking with your paradigm." I say this now when I'm speaking with people who are making excuses and caving to their self-limiting beliefs. Most people laugh and tell me I'm correct.

Bob also spoke about the Six Faculties of the Mind:

1. Perception
2. The Will
3. Imagination
4. Memory
5. Reason
6. Intuition

Humans are the only ones on the planet with these faculties and each one is powerful in and of itself regarding creating what we want in the world, and how we navigate through life.

Bob always carried a Goal Card in his pocket. Whatever Bob's goal was, at any time in life, he had it written down. According to Bob, he explained that the reason he kept it in his pocket was because when he touched it, it was confirming it's importance to his subconscious mind. Then the subconscious mind can get to work having him meet his goal.

After reading *Think and Grow Rich*, learning about the "Stickperson," and what we can do with our marvelous mind, Bob went on to make millions of dollars a year. He didn't fully understand why, so he closed his global corporate office cleaning business and went to go work with Earl Nightengale and Lloyd Conant in Chicago to figure out how he was doing this. They became Bob's mentors, and he credits both for the inspiration to go on and live his best life teaching and coaching what he learned.

Many personal and professional development leaders focus on one dominant Spiritual Universal Law. For Bob, it is the Law of Vibration. The Law of Attraction is secondary to the primary Law of Vibration. As we saw in the movie, *The Secret*, where Bob was a main speaker, we attract to us the people, places, and things we manifest. The experiences, based on our frequency, the rate of our vibration we emit, good or bad, are what we are manifesting and most people on the planet don't know this. When you do begin to understand this, you've become empowered and not easily controlled. They won't teach this in school.

This is the secret to life. We get to choose what kind of a mindset we want and that will determine with absolute certainty our results, the kind of life we live out. The great thing about this is that we can change our mindset at any time, whenever we want.

Bob always said, "If you can hold it in your head, you can hold it in your hand." What he meant by that is, if you can hold a picture in your imagination long enough and bring it alive—taste the food on the table, hear the laughter of those around you, feel the hugs, smell the perfume and cologne, see the vibrant colors—it must objectify itself in the outer world. Thoughts become things. What is impressed in the subconscious mind must express itself in the outer world. It is Law. I tell my kids all the time, "What you think about and speak about you bring about. Guard your thoughts and words very carefully."

Bob said the best thing to happen to his company, one of the largest and most influential coaching companies on the planet for personal and professional development, was when he partnered with Sandy Gallagher in 2006. Sandy, a prominent Wall Street attorney at that time, attended one of Bob's three-day seminars and she said, "It was like Bob took off my head, shook it around, and put it back on again." She started to see life very differently and knew right away that she wanted to be Bob's closest advisor. And she became exactly that and then some. They have a powerful partnership and a beautiful friendship.

I was asked to join the Proctor Gallagher team mid 2023 and I absolutely love it. Bob, Sandy, and our amazing team teach so much of what I've been teaching as a Global Leading Life Coach and Business Strategist for over thirty years. I feel blessed to be part of this prominent company.

I came across Bob Proctor's work in 1991 with a cancer diagnosis, Non-Hodgkins Lymphoblastic Lymphoma, at the young age of 25. I credit these teachings and my application of them for curing me of the cancer when the doctors kept telling me I was going to die. After the grueling two-and-a-half-year protocol ended, I went on to have three children the doctors swore would never happen. The doctors called me The Miracle Maker and started having their patients call me at home.

That's how I started life coaching in the nineties. I implemented what I learned from Bob and many other greats in personal development when going through a tumultuous divorce and growing my business. As a result of learning what Bob has taught me, I am living my best life! I am a conscious creator, and I want that for you, too. Feel free to contact me at *www.ErinLey.com* if you're interested in coaching.

Thank you, Bob Proctor, for your love, warmth, and wisdom. Thank you for passionately simplifying Spiritual Universal Law for the masses who have gone on to create wonderful experiences in life. Thank you for the incredible company you've built with Sandy, who is now at the helm and doing an amazing job.

We can never outperform our self-image; nonetheless, as you have always said, we can work at increasing it daily, leaving fear, worry, and self-doubt behind. You were a bright light here on Earth and I'm certain you're shining even brighter in Heaven. God bless you!

ERIN LEY

About Erin Ley: As Founder and CEO of Onward Productions, Inc., Erin Ley has spent the last 30 years as an Author, Professional Speaker, Personal and Professional Empowerment and Success Coach predominantly around mindset, vision and decision. Founder of many influential summits, including "Life On Track," Erin is also the host of the upcoming online streaming T.V. show, "Life On Track with Erin Ley," which is all about helping you get into the driver's seat of your own life.

They call Erin "The Miracle Maker!" As a cancer survivor at age 25, single mom of 3 at age 47, successful entrepreneur at age 50, Erin has shown thousands upon thousands across the globe how to become victorious by being focused, fearless, and excited about life and your future! Erin says, "Celebrate life and you'll have a life worth celebrating!"

To see more about Erin and the release of her 4th book, *WorkLuv: A Love Story*, along with her "Life On Track" Course & Coaching Programs, please visit her website.

Author's Website: *www.ErinLey.com*

Book Series Website: *www.TheBookOfMentors.com*

FRED MOSKOWITZ

LEVERAGING THE AMAZING POWER OF DECISION

One of the most powerful strengths that we can develop is the ability to make decisions quickly. A common trait found among many successful leaders and high performing individuals is that of decision. The benefits of decision are endless—wealth creation, relationships, goal achievement, health and wellness, and so much more. The result is extraordinary success in life.

As we honor the legacy and impact of the teachings of Bob Proctor in this book volume, I would like to shine a light in this chapter on the amazing power of decision. This is a subject that Bob Proctor has spoken about and taught about on very many occasions.

> *"Successful people make decisions quickly and firmly. Unsuccessful people make decisions slowly, and they change them often."*
> ~ Napoleon Hill

How can we get better at making decisions, and at making them quickly with confidence? Developing the skill of decision is much like developing your muscles by working out at the gym.

Another analogy is that of sharpening a knife through grinding and honing the edge of the steel blade. It is a skill which takes steady and consistent practice to develop, and there certainly are no short cuts or cheat codes. As we put in the hard work to build this skill, it results in powerful and impactful personal growth. And, this growth impacts endless facets of our business and our personal lives.

Key Elements of Making Decisions

Below are some of my favorite elements which go into effective decision making:

Confidence – One of the key ingredients in making decisions. Confidence comes from having a healthy self-image, along with a good self-esteem. Additionally, it is an energy which comes through in our presence, and because of this it is quite impactful to those around us.

Creativity – A unique skill that can work hand in hand with decision making. Creativity can inspire new ideas, new approaches, and new options and choices.

Resourcefulness – Using the knowledge and information you have at that exact moment, to help guide you in your decision making. Better decisions are made by leveraging this ability to use clever and novel approaches to overcome obstacles.

Asking for help – In particular, asking for help from people that are successful and experienced in the context of the topic of the decision. Mentors or experienced colleagues can be a great source of ideas, feedback, suggestions, and wisdom.

Intuition – Trusting the intuitive approach is another key element. One tactic that I like to utilize when making decisions is to do a quick gut-check, allowing us to take into consideration the intuitive feelings in the gut. Consider the possible outcome of a decision that you are facing, and then look forward into the future. What will life be like later on after having made the decision? Think about how you will feel about the decision in 10 days, 10 months, and 10 years. This allows you to take into account your feelings and emotions, which certainly have an important role in the influence on our decisions.

The Archenemy of Decision: Analysis Paralysis

For some people, when it comes time to make a decision, the problem of analysis paralysis shows up as an unwelcome guest to the party, rendering them unable to make a decision. This often happens as a result of having too many things to focus on and there is simply a lack of attention.

The best way to attack this issue is to list everything out written on a piece of paper, and then proceed to rank or weight the elements in order of importance. This way, we can utilize a systematic method of scoring and weighting things so that we can solely focus on the top items.

After the top items have been addressed, we can then take another pass at the less important items and consider them in a secondary manner in the decision-making process. The end result—a solid decision is reached with supporting elements and facts to back it up.

Sharing My Early Experiences of Developing the Skill of Decision

My father taught me his favorite decision-making process to utilize for more complex decisions, which originally came from one of the founding fathers of The United States, Benjamin Franklin. This is a practice that I watched my father execute so many times. He pulled out a sheet of paper, drew a vertical line down the middle of the page, and then together we started listing out the pros on one side, and the cons on the other side.

We talked through each point, reflecting the impact being made from the decision that was being considered. Executing on this process resulted in a mini-brainstorming session which has taken into consideration the various points, possibilities, and impacts. In the end, we arrived at a solid decision that we felt confident about.

"In any moment of decision, the best thing you can do is the right thing.
The worst thing you can do is nothing."
~ Theodore Roosevelt

Conclusion

In this chapter, we have discussed the incredible power and benefits that can be afforded by having the skill of decision. When we make good decisions quickly, it results in improved productivity, more optimal use of resources, and it saves us time. Because of this, it becomes important that we work diligently in order to build up this skill on a daily basis.

By focusing on the key elements of making decisions, we can build a daily practice which allows us to grow and become more skillful decision makers over time. To those who are dedicated and willing to put in the hard work, the results will pay off handsomely in the long run.

FRED MOSKOWITZ

About Fred Moskowitz: Fred Moskowitz is a Best-Selling Author, investment fund manager, and speaker who is on a personal mission to teach people about the power of investing in alternative asset classes, such as real estate and mortgage notes, showing them the way to diversify their capital into investments that are uncorrelated from Wall Street and the stock markets.

Through his body of work, he is teaching investors the strategies to build passive income and cash flow streams designed to flow into their bank accounts. He's a frequent event speaker and contributor to investment podcasts.

Fred is the author of *The Little Green Book of Note Investing: A Practical Guide for Getting Started with Investing in Mortgage Notes* and contributing author in *1Habit To Thrive in a Post-Covid World.*

Author's Website: *www.FredMoskowitz.com*

Book Series Website: *www.TheBookOfMentors.com*

"THE ONLY LIMITS IN OUR LIFE ARE THOSE WE IMPOSE ON OURSELVES."

~ BOB PROCTOR

HYUN MARTIN

CULTIVATING COMMUNITY: UNSEEN MENTORSHIP

My vision is centered on gratitude, choice, and the ability to edit the story of life. It involves reframing your perspective and taking empowering actions to create the world you want to live in. By being the change, you wish to see, you can take steps towards building a better world.

My Journey to Empowerment: A Mosaic of Gratitude & Choice

In the quiet moments of reflection, as I consider the intricate web of experiences that define my life, I am deeply moved by a sense of gratitude. It's my gratitude for the paths I've traversed, for the choices I've made, and for the remarkable capacity to reshape my narrative. This isn't merely about being thankful; it's about recognizing that every thought, every action, is a powerful stroke in the art of creating the world I envision—a world where we can all be agents of the change we seek.

My story, much like the farm I dream of returning to, is deeply rooted in resilience—a resilience borne out of confronting traumas that too many share in silence. The beauty of my vision, the very essence of my drive to foster community and sustainable living, springs from a place of profound personal upheaval.

The Shadows of My Childhood

The trauma of my youth is a shadow that trails behind the light of my endeavors. I was raised on a farm in Texas, surrounded by the rustic charm of Shetland ponies, quarter horses, and the life cycle that brought food from pasture to plate. But this idyllic setting was marred by the disruptive caregiving of my adoptive parents—my uncle, a pedophile, and his complicit wife.

My biological parents, whom I met later in life, brought with them their own complexities. This dual legacy of trauma has made movements like "Me Too" deeply personal. It has sharpened my awareness of the darker facets of human society—where children are commodities, and governments and agencies, swayed by politics and war, too often turn a blind eye to the suffering and exploitation under their care.

Reframing the Narrative

Despite these shadows, or perhaps because of them, I've learned the power of reframing my narrative. I've learned to embrace the farm-to-table ethos not just as a business model but as a way of life—a full circle that honors the natural rhythms of the land and life. It's why I've found myself drawn to creating a unified community through farm-to-table hotels and restaurants. It's an aspiration to provide sustainable living and working environments where creativity thrives and both work and nature nourish the soul.

This vision is fueled by a belief in the importance of a support system—a community that shares in the joys and sorrows of life, something that Western living often neglects. The goal is to foster intergenerational care and sharing, allowing us to age in place and learn from the natural cycle of life.

The Seeds of Legacy and Adaptation

My mother's silent defiance in bringing Korean seeds into the United States, tucked into the folds of her clothing, sowed the seeds of legacy and adaptation. Watercrest, which she grew in a pond due to its water-heavy nature, and the Korean peppers—two varieties that became the bedrock of her sundried red pepper legacy—were more than just crops; they were symbols of resilience and a lifeline to our heritage.

These seeds, these plants, represent a connection to the cycles that govern life itself. Living detached from the environment the seasons, means missing out on a natural rhythm—a rhythm that ties us to both lunar and solar orientations. My parents understood the delicate dance between embracing these cycles and the Western mindset of storage efficiency, creating a balance that integrated the best of both worlds.

A Hug for the World: A Gift for Healing Trauma

And in this tapestry of mentorship and legacy, I have woven my own unique thread—my famous hug. It is more than a simple embrace; it's a symbol of connection and the warmth of community that I strive to create in every aspect of my life. It is my gift to the world, embodying the unseen mentorship that has been my guiding light.

My mission is to help people recover from trauma with my famous hug. It is both scientific and energetic, and it only takes 20 seconds. The safest way to embrace is to align left to left, from heart to heart, with the right arm over the left. Hold each other and take deep breaths, breathing in and out of your stomach. As you exhale, make an audible sigh, and the other person will follow suit. This will synchronize your hearts and create a harmonic field. Repeat three times and exhale twice as long as you inhale to activate the parasympathetic nervous system.

To add to the experience, you can also use sounds like "aw," "om," "moo," or "yum" to enhance the effect of the hug. "Aw" is for primal screaming, "om" is for spiritual connection, "moo" is for laughter, and "yum" is for love. These sounds create a resonant field that amplifies the experience of the hug.

People who are too shy to sing in public can instead hum, but the effects are less powerful than using the sounds above. I encourage everyone to learn the value of hugs and to become ambassadors for this practice. Embracing pain can relieve hormones, and allowing people into your field can create a sense of safety. Most people are touch-deprived, and this hug can change that. It is both energetic and experiential, and you can even hear the voices that create resonance.

The Unseen Threads of Mentorship

As I contemplate buying a farm and building a community, I am keenly aware that the mentorship that has shaped me is seen and unseen. It's in the very land that sustains us, in the rhythms of nature that we've been taught to honor, and in the life lessons passed down through generations. My adoptive and biological parents, despite their flaws, have inadvertently mentored me through the contrast of their lives and the resilience they've embedded in my spirit.

Their legacies, marred by human frailties yet rich in lessons, highlight the power of unseen mentorship—the kind that doesn't come with accolades or public recognition. It's the mentorship that comes from life's trials, from the hard-earned wisdom of experience, and from the silent heroes who live among us.

It is this mentorship that has shown me that we all possess an innate potential for greatness and we are all capable of making a positive impact on the world. It reminds us that our darkest moments can give birth to the brightest futures if we choose to weave them into our story with intention and courage.

And so, as I stand at the precipice of my next chapter, I am filled with a sense of hope. For in every ending lies the promise of a new beginning—a chance to plant new seeds, cultivate new growth, and contribute to the ever-evolving tapestry of our shared human experience

HYUN MARTIN

About Hyun Martin: Hyun Martin, a world-class chef, healer, and influential community leader, has made a profound impact through her diverse roles as a spa owner, trainer, author, and coach. Born in Incheon, Korea, Hyun has cultivated a rich background in holistic wellness and culinary arts, studying at Indiana University and dedicating over a 50-year journey of delving into transpersonal psychology, human potential movement, community development leadership, and East-West integration.

As the founder of Be You Bi Yu Wellness Center & Spa, Hyun has created a transformative space that merges beauty, health, and wellness, complemented by a retail store to enhance conscious living. Hyun's commitment to community development is evident through her role as a Community Development Coordinator at LIGHT OF TRUTH CENTER INC, where she advocates for mental health, addiction recovery, and corporate sponsorships. Her passion for mentorship and healing extends to her work as a Certified Inner Alignment Coach, drawing inspiration from the "Kintsugi" Art of the Soul.

A published author and dedicated mompreneur, Hyun has shared her personal journey and insights in her memoir *I Survived Childhood: A Memoir of Abandonment, Betrayal and Healing*, and is a co-author and publisher for the upcoming *Asian American Anthology: I am an American Too*. Her commitment to love over fear and hate, combined with her advocacy for trauma survivors as a #MeTooCSA TRA, underscores her dedication to creating a world grounded in compassion, understanding, and holistic well-being.

Author's Website: *www.HyunMartin.com*

Book Series Website: *www.TheBookOfMentors.com*

JEFFREY LEVINE

THE PARADIGM SHIFT

Paradigms

Most peoples' challenge is they go on in life living as Lone Rangers. They're doing everything themselves, and we all have blind spots. We all have paradigms, which Bob Proctor mentioned in his seminars and books. For the first time in my career in self-development, in 2017, he spoke about that, and I had never heard the word before. But it's so powerful. Paradigms are a mental program because of your conditioning to keep you comfortable and in the same place, not to let you grow.

In my career as a financial planner and tax attorney for 32 years, I had this little voice when I had a new opportunity that kept saying, "You're not good enough. This is risky. This will never work. Who do you think you are?" And I never said yes for 32 years because I didn't understand what was happening. There are so many people out there who don't understand paradigms.

If Bob Proctor was the only one talking about it at the time, that's a small percentage of the people who have heard of this concept. So, you have a paradigm that will talk you out of almost everything. You need to understand that this is what will happen every time. I tell my clients before they make a decision that they're going to run up against this strong paradigm, telling them not to do it, it's risky, it's not going to work, you're wasting your money—but if they know that beforehand, and they have a strong enough desire, they can overcome that paradigm. That's what I preach: the desire to make it is so strong that it overcomes the paradigm. And if you don't know, it's easy for that paradigm to take control.

"A paradigm is a mental program that has almost exclusive control over our habitual behavior...and almost all of our behavior is habitual."
~ Bob Proctor

Regretfully, most people don't have a strong desire or the need to overcome the paradigm. So that's what I teach in my Thinking into Results Course with Bob Proctor. You have to know some of the other principles to get around it; if you don't, the paradigm wins, and nothing changes when the paradigm wins. You don't grow. I need to find out how many people are stuck, and the word "stick" means paradigm. They don't know that that's what it is. And they keep searching and working harder, and it doesn't work because they get burnt out, and then they're back to nothing. They're out of work. They can't do anything.

Belief & Capability

It's time to understand the paradigm so you can move forward. When that next opportunity comes, instead of saying, "I'm not good enough. I don't deserve that. I can't do that," say a new word: "I can. I can." As Henry Ford said, "If you think you can or feel you can't, either way, you're right." And if you think you can, you will find a way.

"If you see it in your mind, you will hold it in your hand."
~ Bob Proctor

Decision-making is the most important thing, and it is something that most people need to talk about. You're never taught in school how to make a decision. You're never taught that in real life. Making a decision changes everything. What people don't know and think they should know is that once you make a decision, all the things you need to follow through on that decision will show up.

But most people think, "I have to do this. When the kids get through school, I'll do it. I'll buy the car next year when I get my bonus." And that doesn't work because something will come up between that time that will derail you and throw you off. In making a decision, the most successful thing about making a decision, if you think of all the most successful people, is that they make a decision fast, and they don't let their paradigm take control. But if you do it fast, the paradigm doesn't show up. I always say to decide within 5 seconds.

That voice went off when I didn't decide in my financial planning and tax attorney practice within about 7 or 8 seconds. So, you have to beat that. And if you don't, you're back in the same place; there's no growth.

Think of all the great people out there, the successful people in the world. They don't sit back and gather information; they do the opposite. They take action and then gather information. So, one of the statements I always use, instead of "Aim, fire!" I say "Fire, fire, and fire!" and then I'll aim afterward.

Impression of Increase

One of my favorite things is the "Impression of Increase." Bob Proctor emphasized the power of positive energy and influence: "Always leave people with the impression of increase." How do you talk to somebody without making them feel better? It's all about making them feel better. It's about a compliment! Simply recognize them as a critical person, and admire all the help they give you.

For example, I never thought I'd have so many Amazon number one best-selling books. I would only have one working with Erik Swanson, but I now have several. We'll be up to 17 at some point soon. How exciting to meet other people as book authors and who they are! And that is so important. However, the most important thing beyond paradigms is attitude. Now, you think, "Oh, I have a good attitude," but you have a good attitude when things are good. How's your attitude when things are not so good? Not quite as good?

"Action is the bridge between the inner world and the outer world."
~ Bob Proctor

A Positive Self-Image

"You are the only problem you will ever have and you are the only solution."
~ Bob Proctor

For many of us in our upbringing, including myself, our self-image was never that good. I was always told, "No, you can't. Who do you think you are?" And I didn't. The bottom line is that you cannot outperform your self-image, but you can change it.

One thing Bob Proctor is known for doing beyond the other things I've talked about is improving self-image. And what we do to improve our self-image is we take the self-image of the person we admire, of the person who's doing what we want to do, and write out a script. You write that script exactly how that person is and what you want to be. If that person is an action taker, I am an action taker. If they use the impression of increase, I'm an impression of increase. But they all have a positive attitude, too. So, you write up a script about a page long, and on that page, you read it every 3 hours, record it repeatedly, and you're reprogramming your self-image.

Goals (A, B, & C Goals)

"Set a goal to achieve something that is so big, so exhilarating that it excites you and scares you at the same time."
~ Bob Proctor

You can become a different person and become more successful. But people need to figure out what to do. The last thing I want to talk about is goal setting. Bob recommends doing something called the ABC goals. The A goal is something I already know how to do. For example, if I bought a Ford four years ago and I want a new Ford, I already know how to do it. I did it once.

The second type of goal is a B goal. The B goal is, if everything goes right, I can do it. I'm supposed to get a bonus next year. If I get that bonus, the kids will be off from school, and everybody will be healthy; I can reach my B goal and take the trip. But the C goal is different.

The C goal is the exciting goal. It's a goal that you've never done before. And here's how I phrase it: it excites and scares you simultaneously. Now, to go for a C goal, you need to relax, and let your imagination run, and you will come up with things you want to do.

You should always have two types of goals: a personal and then a professional goal. And then the secret is you write out a goal card. This card reminds you, "I am so happy and grateful that I wrote down my goal. Whatever it is, it's already done." And when something's already done, you have that emotional feeling of excitement and keep repeating it every 3 to 4 hours daily.

But the most critical time is when you first wake up. That's when your subconscious is wide open, and you read the goal for 1 minute and visualize 1 minute each goal every 3 hours. But the most critical time again is before you go to sleep—get that mind percolating all night.

I gave a seminar, and somebody who was very well-schooled and thriving in the audience said, "I never heard anybody talking about doing it on the first of the morning or at night." She said, "I'm going to have the most phenomenal 2024 that I ever had," and she's already successful. But now she's got the recipe for the pie or the cake, and the opportunity for her now is incredible.

"Take responsibility for your life. Know that it is you who will get you where you want to go, no one else."
~ Bob Proctor

It was strange. I had heard of every other mentor except Bob. Here it is, 2017. I've been on a journey since 1985 and had never heard his name. My partner had always been going to his seminars in LA for years and years. Well, there was one time he couldn't go, and it started Friday night, went Saturday and Sunday, and he called me and said, "I have a ticket for Bob Proctor." I remember the words, "I would hate to waste the ticket."

And I'm a guy that says, "Yes, done, I don't want you to waste the ticket. I'm going."

It was in LA at a Sheridan or a Hilton. I couldn't remember what it was, and I walked in. Who was Bob Proctor? I mean, I didn't even know why I was there. Within an hour, I was mesmerized. Here's this guy, 80 years old, teaching me stuff I had never heard of before. For two and a half days, I was mesmerized. The place was fully packed, and I went on a journey. I took all his courses, every single course he had. I read every book he had many times and studied every day 3 for 5 hours of his programs. I took his coaching and attended every seminar he attended. I went every three months until he passed away.

What's different about Bob is that he understands the mind, the conscious, and the subconscious. But the difference with Bob is that he can teach you to reprogram the subconscious. The paradigm is in the subconscious, so you need to reprogram it. Otherwise, the paradigm will control you. His seminar's name was A Paradigm Shift. You have to shift the paradigm. Even though he's passed, his partner, Sandy Gallagher, is doing some of the best training I've ever heard, even better than what Bob was doing. I am blessed. I am grateful. Even though Bob Proctor's not here, his legacy is.

The Stick Man (Conscious & Subconscious)

Bob taught something called the Stick Man. Even though nobody understood the mind, one of the people he knew even drew a picture of the mind, and he's always called it the stick man. Bob uses the Stick Man concept to illustrate how thoughts control our actions and results. Bob often said, "Thoughts become things. If you see it in your mind, you will hold it in your hand."

I think this is the single best idea I've ever heard. Once you understand the stick man, you will never get stuck. A picture is worth a thousand words, but he teaches that the conscious mind is the thinking mind, and the conscious mind allows you to have a choice: what comes to your conscious mind can be accepted or rejected. But the subconscious mind, and I can't say this enough, accepts everything.

So, whenever you take a negative thing, that subconscious mind is getting it, and that's deprogramming you. The first order of business is to focus on your thinking. What are you letting in? The most important thing is to reject what doesn't serve you and accept what serves you. Then, the subconscious mind has to reprogram it in repetition, repetition, repetition, over and over until that one day, you've made that paradigm shift. That's the most potent idea Bob's ever had, and it's the most powerful idea I've ever had.

JEFFREY LEVINE

About Jeffrey Levine: Jeffrey is a highly skilled tax planner and business strategist, as well as a published author and sought-after speaker. He's been featured in national magazines, on the cover of *Influential People Magazine*, and is a frequent featured expert on radio, talk shows, and documentaries. Jeffrey attended the prestigious Albany Academy for high school and then went on to the University of Hartford at Connecticut, the University of Mississippi Law School, and Boston University School of Law, and earned an L.L.M. in taxation. His accolades include features in Kiplinger and Family Circle Magazine, as well as a dedicated commentator for Channel 6 and 13 news shows, a contributor for the *Albany Business Review*, and a talk show host for WGY Radio.

Jeffrey has accumulated more than 30 years of experience as a tax attorney and certified financial planner and has given in excess of 500 speeches nationally. Levine is the executive producer and cast member in the documentary *Beyond the Secret: The Awakening*.

Levine's most current work, Consistent Profitable Growth Map, is a step-by-step workbook outlining easy-to-follow steps to convert consistent revenue growth to any business platform.

Author's Website: *www.Strategies.org*

Book Series Website: *www.TheBookOfMentors.com*

JON KOVACH JR.

HEROES ARE REMEMBERED, BUT LEGENDS NEVER DIE

"You have within you right now, everything you need to deal with whatever the world can throw at you."
~ **Bob Proctor**

I remember exactly where I was the day it happened. I was leaving my place in Midway, Utah, to go to my office. There were a dozen boxes of books on my doorstep. We had just published our newest #1 bestseller book and my bulk order of copies was piled on my porch. As I quickly and excitedly loaded those boxes into my front room, I received a notification on my phone, which took my attention away from the mid-year Christmas presents I had just received. Yes, getting our books always feels like Christmas. I love the sensory experience of opening up that first box of books. I love to thumb through the pages, smell the books, and put my face on the cover like a brand-new pillow. It is one of those bucket-list experiences anyone who desires to become an author should experience for themselves.

Holding your creation and flipping through the pages filled with your thoughts and ideas is indescribable. It's a moment of pure joy and accomplishment, a tangible representation of all the hard work and dedication to crafting those words into a cohesive piece of art. Each book is like a piece of your soul bound in paper and ink, ready to be shared with the world.

As I distractedly grabbed my phone from my pocket to check the notifications, I nearly dropped it when I read the message's subject line that broke through to my notifications. It read, "Bob Proctor passed away at age 87…" My heart sank. It felt like I had just lost a family member. But Bob was not, nor did Bob ever know that I existed.

I sat there momentarily, trying to process the unexpected news of Bob Proctor's passing. Though I had never met him, his wisdom and guidance profoundly touched my life. His words had been a source of inspiration and motivation during some of my darkest days. Bob's teachings have helped me believe in the power of my thoughts and the importance of setting clear goals. As I reflected on his legacy, I realized that even in his physical absence, his impact on the world would continue to live on through the countless lives he had touched. I silently vowed to honor his memory by continuing to apply his teachings in my own life and sharing his wisdom with others. In that moment of reflection, I felt a sense of gratitude for having crossed paths with such a remarkable individual, even if it was only through his words.

The Impact of Virtual Mentors

How could someone I never met have such an impact on me?

I picked up my first copy of Think and Grow Rich by Napoleon Hill in 2016. That led to exploring entrepreneurism, leaving my 9-to-5 corporate job, diving into various masterminds, and venturing down a path and adventure that has taken me here to the present. Naturally, when you find a work of art as monumental and transformational as Think and Grow Rich, I researched experts and mentors in the Think-And-Grow-Rich world to deepen my research, expand my knowledge, and become an expert. Of all the names, one of the first ones that popped up was Bob Proctor. As I delved deeper into his teachings and philosophy, I was captivated by his wisdom and unique approach to personal growth.

Learning from Bob Proctor expanded my understanding of the principles outlined in Think and Grow Rich. It provided me with practical tools and strategies to implement in my journey toward success. His emphasis on the power of the mind, visualization techniques, and the importance of setting clear goals resonated deeply with me, igniting a new-found sense of purpose and determination.

Embracing Bob Proctor's teachings has transformed my mindset and catalyzed significant growth in various aspects of my life. Through his guidance, I have cultivated a greater sense of self-awareness, harnessed the law of attraction to manifest my desires, and developed a resilient mindset capable of overcoming any obstacle that comes my way.

As I continue to walk the path paved by the invaluable lessons of Think and Grow Rich and Bob Proctor's teachings, I am grateful for their transformative impact on my life. With each passing day, I am inspired to reach new heights, unlock my full potential, and create the life of abundance and fulfillment that I have always envisioned. Bob Proctor's legacy shines brightly as a guiding light for those seeking to embark on their own personal and professional growth journey.

A title that struck a chord with me, because I wasn't sure at that moment whether it complimented or contradicted my new-found love for Think and Grow Rich, was a book titled *Born Rich* by Bob Proctor. Instantly, I bought that book and began another well-researched rabbit hole of information that compounded my foundational beliefs necessary to becoming "rich." My goal is to become rich, but it's deeper than that. I wanted to live an abundant life so I could serve and help more people.

I delved into the pages of *Born Rich* with eager anticipation, hungry for Bob Proctor's wisdom and insights. As I journeyed through the book, I was captivated by Proctor's perspective on wealth and abundance. It wasn't just about amassing material riches; it was about cultivating a mindset of prosperity and abundance in all aspects of life.

Proctor's teachings resonated with me profoundly, stirring a new-found sense of purpose and possibility within me. I realized that true richness extended far beyond mere financial wealth; it encompassed a holistic abundance that touched every facet of existence.

Armed with this new-found understanding, I embarked on a transformative journey towards creating a life of boundless prosperity and fulfillment. With each page turned and each lesson absorbed, I felt myself inching closer to the vibrant, abundant life I envisioned.

As I closed the book, I knew that my pursuit of richness was not merely a quest for wealth but a quest for a life brimming with joy, purpose, and prosperity in all its forms. Bob Proctor's words had ignited a fire within me, illuminating a path toward a future teeming with abundance and possibility.

I later discovered that Bob Proctor and many other enthusiastic leaders had aligned their beliefs and personal development modalities with the Think and Grow Rich model. I finally found my business bible, foundation, and roots to becoming the leader I have always felt drawn and called to. The lineage of leaders stemming from Think and Grow Rich has branched out to many realms and areas of work and industries. But Bob was different.

Bob Proctor stood out for his wealth of knowledge, experience, and unique ability to inspire and uplift others. His teachings went beyond financial success and encompassed a holistic personal growth and fulfillment approach.

Bob's message was clear and powerful: success is not just about material wealth but about achieving harmony in all aspects of life. His words guided me as I navigated my journey towards becoming a better version of myself. With each lesson learned and each insight gained, I felt myself transforming into the leader I had always envisioned.

Perpetuating A Legacy Like Bob's

What Bob Proctor accomplished in his lifetime speaks volumes about my dream of building something significant enough to outlive me. In many of my published work and writings, I often admit that growing up all I ever wanted to be was a respected professional who helped a significant number of people.

I wanted to make a mark in the world, to leave a legacy that would inspire others long after I'm gone. In every word I write and every project I undertake, I strive to create something that will stand the test of time, resonate with people, and positively impact the world. Each step toward my goals reminds me of the power of perseverance, passion, and purpose. And I know that as long as I stay true to my vision and keep pushing forward, I, too, can build something great that will endure far beyond my lifetime.

At first, I thought that path was an Olympic athlete. Then, I transitioned to the world of communications and public relations. That all ultimately led to a new-found calling to bring Napoleon Hill's Mastermind Methodologies to every corner of the earth, where every person and professional can tap into its practical functionality, accelerate results, and solve problems and challenges in any area of life and business.

Embracing the teachings of Napoleon Hill's Mastermind Methodologies has been a transformative journey for this individual. Through their expertise in communications, they have found a new passion for spreading the wisdom that can be gleaned from Hill's methods. By sharing these powerful strategies, they aim to empower individuals from all walks of life to unlock their full potential and succeed in personal and professional endeavors. With dedication and a genuine desire to make a positive impact, they are on a mission to inspire others to leverage these methodologies for growth, problem-solving, and success in every facet of their lives.

My dream and vision became so clear that my impact and legacy would be teaching millions worldwide how conducting the Mastermind Methodologies in any scenario and aspect of your life can lead to exponentially positive outcomes.

Imagine a world where individuals from all walks of life are empowered with the tools and knowledge to apply the Mastermind Methodology to their daily routines. Collaboration, innovation, and strategic thinking combine to create a compounding effect of positivity and success. Picture a community where problems are seen as growth opportunities and challenges are embraced as modalities towards a brighter future. In this vision, every person can tap into their inner potential and unlock endless possibilities. As we strive to spread this philosophy far and wide, we pave the way for a world where positivity, growth, and success are not just aspirations but a way of life for millions around the globe.

I've tested these methods in both professional and casual environments. I've used them on athletes as a coach, Sunday school youth counselor, and young adult mentor in leadership ministry and stewardship roles. To name some other areas, I've tested these activities and their effectiveness at college game nights, collegiate campus clubs, professional trade organization functions, family dinners, networking events, planning meetings, executive boardrooms, and even at government-level municipal public meetings and gatherings, to name a few. They worked every single time in every function.

I've found that incorporating these methods into various settings has been truly transformative. The impact has been profound, whether interacting with athletes, guiding youth in Sunday school, or mentoring young adults in leadership roles. From college game nights to executive boardrooms, these activities have consistently proven effective in fostering meaningful connections and enhancing outcomes. I firmly believe that embracing these Mastermind Methods has enriched our experiences, deepened our relationships, and elevated our results to levels beyond what we could have imagined.

The mastermind methodologies have been my brain's lightbulb switch for creative thought, which can connect to the ether of ideas and our creative imagination and then tap into personal access to the brilliance and frequency of infinite intelligence. I know that's a mouthful and sort of out-of-this-world thinking, but it is exactly what you begin to see and comprehend about being rich and successful as you empower Think and Grow Rich to transform your belief systems.

But bear with me, as we delve deeper into this concept. Imagine your mind as a vast universe, filled with endless possibilities and untapped potential. By embracing mastermind methodologies, you are essentially unlocking the doors to this universe, allowing your thoughts to flow freely and connect with the boundless realm of creativity. It's like tapping into a wellspring of inspiration, where ideas dance effortlessly, and innovation knows no bounds. So, the next time you feel overwhelmed by the enormity of your ideas, remember that you hold the key to accessing a realm of infinite intelligence within yourself. Embrace the journey, trust in your abilities, and let the brilliance of your imagination guide you towards greatness.

When I first experienced this mastermind phenomenon, I saw the world from a different lens, where it was clear as day that I could possess anything I desired and became as natural as flowing water from a mountain glacier. It was magnificent.

As I continued to embrace this new-found perspective, I realized that the power of manifestation lay within me all along. The ability to attract abundance and positivity into my life simply by aligning my thoughts with my desires was a revelation that brought a sense of liberation and infinite possibilities. Each day became a canvas on which I painted my dreams and aspirations, watching them come to life in vibrant hues of success and fulfillment. The journey of self-discovery and empowerment had just begun, opening doors to a world where the only limits were those of my imagination. And so, with boundless enthusiasm and unwavering faith, I embarked on a thrilling adventure of creating my reality, one beautiful manifestation at a time.

"The greatest discovery of my generation is that a human being can alter his life by altering his attitudes."
~ Bob Proctor

To learn more about Napoleon Hill's Mastermind Methods, simply open your copy of Think and Grow Rich up to chapter 10 and start reading. I've dedicated my life, professional, and mission to helping people experience the mastermind the way I have. I invite everyone to learn more, experience a mastermind, and apply its transformative results in their lives. I've used social media as a platform to educate and teach people about these methods. I am also involved in some of the best masterminds in the world, where professionals come and work on their goals, dreams, and aspirations. I help facilitate a group for Champions (Champion Circle) seeking to win more in their lives and businesses. I help facilitate groups where people from all over the world want to improve their habits, attitudes, and ability to thrive (Habitude Warrior

Mastermind, Global Speakers Mastermind, and Café Mastermind). I also use these methods in almost every aspect of my life because of their effectiveness and intentionality.

Understanding this seemingly fictitious realm was made accessible and tangible by no one other than Bob Proctor. Because of him, I acknowledged my inner desires and beliefs, which led to the destruction of many limiting and negative beliefs I had innately clung to growing up. Bob educated many people and was a steward of the idea that anyone could think and grow rich because they were born rich. I accepted that there is a universe of abundance, and you are waiting for it to be taken and used.

"The only thing that stands between you and your dream is the will to try and the belief that it is actually possible."
~ Bob Proctor

Here's one of the secrets: wealth and success are not limited resources but available to anyone willing to believe in themselves and take inspired action. By shifting my perspective and adopting a more positive outlook, I began to attract opportunities and experiences that aligned with my new-found belief in abundance.

I am forever grateful for Bob Proctor's wisdom and legacy of mentorship. I know that if you simply learn more about what he taught, or dive deeper into understanding Mastermind Methods, you too will have transformational opportunities in your life.

JON KOVACH JR.

About Jon Kovach Jr.: Jon is an award-winning international motivational speaker and global mastermind leader. Jon has helped multi-billion-dollar corporations exceed their annual sales goals, including Coldwell Banker Commercial, Outdoor Retailer Cotopaxi, and the Public Relations Student Society of America. In addition, in his work as an accountability coach and mastermind facilitator, Jon has helped thousands of professionals overcome their challenges and achieve their goals by implementing his accountability strategies and Irrefutable Laws of High Performance. Jon is the Founder and Chairman of Champion Circle, a networking association that combines high-performance-based networking activities and recreational fun to create connection capital and increase prosperity for professionals. Jon is the Mastermind Facilitator and Team Lead of the Habitude Warrior Mastermind and the Global Speakers Mastermind & Masterclass founded by Speaker Erik "Mr. Awesome" Swanson.

Jon speaks on topics including accountability, The Irrefutable Laws of High Performance, and The Power of Mastermind Methodologies. He is a #1 Best-Selling Author and a featured keynote on SpeakUp TV, an Amazon Prime TV series, with his keynote speech titled, Getting Unstuck. In addition, he stars in over 100 speaking stages, podcasts, and live international summits each year. Jon's motivational messages have been viewed by over 300,000 people online. His voice has been used by global brands and creators on TikTok and Instagram Reels, such as: Red Bull USA, Michael Bublé, The NHL, Powell Books, GoDaddy Studio, Canada's Wonderland Amusement Park, and the LSU Cheer Team.

Author's website: *www.SpeakerJonKovachJr.com*
Book Series Website: *www.TheBookOfMentors.com*

JULIE DELGADILLO

JOURNEY TOWARD MY NORTH STAR

"Anyone that ever accomplished anything, did not know how they were going to do it. They only knew they were going to do it."
~ **Bob Proctor**

In 2016, I decided I needed a coach. I had hit a plateau in my career and realized that I had no idea how I was going to reach that level; I just knew it was going to happen.

This time it wasn't just another Google search or binging YouTube videos. I knew I had to do everything differently, make tough decisions, and uncover the parts of me that needed improvement.

As I sat at my desk, I put my head down to pray to God to help me discover what I needed to do. I said my prayer and I did what I always did: I went online shopping. I opened my wallet to make an online purchase for yet another item I didn't need, when my phone rang. I almost sent it to voicemail, but something nudged me to answer it. When I did, I heard, "Juuulliiieee!" in the happiest voice. You see, for over a year, I carried a business card for a Thinking Into Results Coach named Barbara. And believe it or not, her voice still echoed in my head a year later and guess who it was on the phone: Barbara.

I trusted in the timing of her call. I embarked on a journey and worked with Barbara. She helped me to identify the blind spots and all the areas

177

of my life that I could not see for myself. It helped me to begin identifying the patterns that weren't working for me and allowed me to take a closer look at what was keeping me from moving forward and thriving.

That phone call changed everything. Barbara helped me to see myself—the good, the bad, and everything in between, and it set me on my path towards my North Star.

Deep down, I always knew my purpose, but fear held me back from fully embracing it and stepping into my power. I craved guidance and discipline, but what I needed was an unwavering belief in myself and to look within. Through Barbara's guidance, I developed my new self-image and cultivated trust in my abilities.

You see, you and I weren't put on this earth to struggle, be stuck, and live in fear. The Bible reminds us of that 366 times: FEAR NOT! I truly believe we were put on this earth to thrive and make a huge impact in the world and in the lives of others.

And some people are put along our journey to help us do just that. Barbara is one of those people for me. And I am forever grateful for her, because she was my answered prayer.

I am proud of the woman I am today. I now lead with confidence, I have a great self-image, and live on purpose. I continue to embrace the unknown because I am self-aware enough to know there is always another level to discover more of the woman I am becoming, and excited for her evolution.

Remember, the journey is yours for you to discover, but you don't have to take it alone. Find your coach, do the hard work, and let them guide you on your journey towards your North Star, so that you too can go conquer the world. And if you want me to coach you and help you develop your confidence and step into your power, connect with me.

JULIE DELGADILLO

About Julie Delgadillo: Julie Delgadillo is a confident, enthusiastic, witty, and sought-after passionate servant leader and mentor with over 20 years of experience in non-profit management, leadership development, and confidence coaching. Julie is the Executive Director of Corazón U.S. & Mexico. Julie is a firm believer in leading by example and actively engages in developing community leaders. It's not uncommon to catch her rolling up her sleeves and wearing a toolbelt to personally contribute to building homes in Mexico for deserving low-income families.

Julie's strengths and passions are rooted in empowering women to be confidence in every area of their lives. Julie has personally coached and developed teens and women from across the globe and serves as an International Ambassador for the economic development of women. Julie is also a former International Beauty Queen and a long-time Hunger Relief Advocate.

An alumna of the prestigious University of Notre Dame's Mendoza School of Business Non-Profit Business Management Executive Leadership Program, Julie's educational journey is a testament to her commitment to growth and learning. Her undergraduate studies at Mount Saint Mary College and her certification in transformational life coaching from the Life Purpose Institute further enrich her holistic approach to empowerment. When she is not out conquering the world, you can find her discovering new brunch spots, listening to audiobooks, or in the aisles of TJ Maxx, Marshall's, or HomeGoods. Let's Connect: *www.Linkedin.com/in/JulieDelgadillo*

Author's Website: *www.linktr.ee/SheConquersTheWorld*

Book Series Website: *www.TheBookOfMentors.com*

"CHANGE IS INEVITABLE BUT PERSONAL GROWTH IS A CHOICE."

~ BOB PROCTOR

KELLI HUDSON-KEY

FAITH OVER FEAR: FINDING COURAGE IN THE CALL TO CHANGE

. . . .

After the pandemic, I think we are seeing a lot of people who are streamlining into entrepreneurship. Now, more than ever, I believe people are searching for something more, searching for freedom, for increased flexibility, not just higher income. There seems to be more and more people starting their own businesses, becoming professional coaches, business coaches, or authors, and even delving into direct sales.

I have been a work-from-home Mompreneur for over 30 years. Working for yourself is a different ball game than working for a boss. It's definitely not for the faint of heart. It requires an extra-large dosage of daily discipline. You have to get up every day, get dressed, and go to work, even if your work commute is literally from your bedroom to your office or to your kitchen table.

Most importantly, you must treat your business like a business. I work with many people who have never been their own boss. I counsel them, to find what works best for you and not to do things just the way I do things because their story is unique. Your story is your story. You and I don't work the same. We can share ideas and work in a similar arena, but we work differently. When working from home it is often difficult to find work and home life balance because there is always work to be done.

You have to find balance between when to turn it on and when to turn it off. But you do have to show up daily, and that's where the tricky part comes in. That's why people succeed and why they don't. If you treat your business like a business, it will pay you like a business. If you treat your business like a hobby, it will pay you like a hobby.

One of the biggest business challenges for me was changing my role at the age of 55. I felt the struggle of the whole "old dog, new tricks" dilemma. I wasn't sure that at my age I could really start over and step out in faith. I did get a very strong answer from God that it was time to make a change. Being who I am, I kept really questioning God and I just wasn't sure if I was brave enough to take this giant leap of faith. Yep! I questioned God! I'm that girl, but I was just scared to death. Leaving a company after 22 years, where I had a free pink car sitting in my driveway that I would have to give back because I hadn't purchased a car in over 22 years.

Thinking my husband would talk me out of this crazy idea to change direction, at MY age, I shared all of the doubts and concerns with him hoping he would be sensible and tell me I was bonkers. He is the rational, cautious one in the relationship and the analytical of the family. I just thought he would think I had lost my mind and question why I was ready to walk away from everything I had built. I had a large team, a great income, and people who counted on me. I was comfortable and had really settled into my comfort zone. I was scared, literally terrified, to make a change, to step outside of my comfort zone.

Not only did he not talk me out of it, he threw his support behind me and said he thought I was ready to move on. And, oh my gosh, the blessings that have come because I was obedient to what God was calling me to do and willing to risk myself and try. Of course, this should not be a surprise, because God was in control the whole time and He already had the details worked out. Funny how that works, isn't it?

I have not regretted this new direction for one single moment. I have spoken from a world platform to thousands of people with my company. I have traveled the world, visiting Europe three times in my first 18 months in my new role. All pinch-me moments. One of my fondest memories is when I took my 80-year-old Mom to Rome with me. She had never been to Europe and sadly she passed away a year later. Those are memories of a lifetime all because I was willing to risk it all and trust God and all that was in store for me. I was playing small, and I didn't realize it. He was like, "Oh no, there's a bigger arena for you. There's so much more that you have to offer." It was time to slam the door and move on. So, that's exactly what I did.

My daughter recently left her position, her paid salaried position with a prominent company. She's been in television and film production her whole professional career. And she just stepped out in faith so she and her husband can start their own film production and marketing company here in Texas. It's scary, but on the other side, it's so exciting. And you must ask yourself, what's the worst that can happen? You can work hard to build someone else's dream or work hard to build your own. Why not make your own?

Life is always going to get in the way. Do you want to try, or do you want always to wonder what if? People often ask, what if it doesn't work out? I always ask, what if it does? You're going to be in control of your own destiny, have creative control, income control, and all these things you want, and be able to design the life you love, not let someone else design it based on their needs and income. You get to create it.

I also believe strongly that where much is given, much is required. It's so important to teach others how to serve humankind, how to find that attitude of gratitude, to be grateful for all that you have, and then be generous with that success. The best way to succeed is to teach others what you have learned.

Serving others and having an attitude of gratitude are key. It's about being generous with your success and teaching others what you've learned. This not only enriches your life but those around you. My life's changes, especially at 55, were a leap of faith, and it turned out to be the best decision, filled with blessings and opportunities I never imagined. It's a testament to not playing it small, listening to that inner call, and stepping into a larger arena where I could offer much more.

This journey has taught me the importance of not waiting, stepping out even when scared, and of the immense potential on the other side of fear. I hope to pass on to others the importance of pursuing your dreams, stepping out in faith, and never settling for less than you can achieve.

My transition wasn't just about a career change; it symbolized a shift in mindset, from fear to faith, from comfort to courage. Looking back, the decision to leave a stable position wasn't just about seeking better opportunities—it was about obeying a more profound calling and embracing the unknown with trust. This leap of faith wasn't just a personal victory; it became a powerful narrative I could share to inspire others to chase their dreams, regardless of their age or stage in life.

This narrative transcends my story, reflecting a universal theme of growth and transformation. It's about breaking free from the shackles of comfort and the familiar to embrace a path aligned with one's authentic self and divine purpose. This journey has shown me that true fulfillment lies not in the accolades or achievements but in the courage to pursue a path that resonates with one's soul, even when it defies logic or societal expectations.

Despite the fears and uncertainties, my daughter's bold move to leave her job and start her own company is a testament to the power of belief and the courage to follow one's dreams. It's a narrative that should be shared more widely encouraging others, especially women, to take ownership of their destinies and dare to dream big. Much like mine, her journey is a reminder that the most significant risk is not in failing but in never attempting, in letting the 'what ifs' define our choices.

The lessons learned from these experiences are manifold:

1. Listening to that inner voice, the divine nudge that guides us toward our true calling is essential.
2. The significance of stepping out in faith, trusting that the path will unfold as we take the first step.
3. The realization that our greatest contributions often lie just beyond our comfort zones, in the realms we're initially afraid to explore.

As I reflect on this journey, I'm reminded of the ripple effect of our actions. By choosing faith over fear and daring to follow our dreams, we transform our lives and inspire others to do the same. It's about creating a legacy of courage, of a life lived true to one's calling, and of the indomitable spirit that refuses to settle for anything less than its fullest potential.

In sharing my story, I hope to ignite a spark in others and awaken them to their potential and possibilities. It's a call to action to live boldly and authentically, embrace the challenges as opportunities for growth, and always remember that it's never too late to pursue your dreams. With all its fears and uncertainties, this journey has been the most rewarding adventure of my life, and it's a message I'm passionate about sharing with the world.

The essence of my story, and the stories like mine, is not merely about career changes or taking leaps of faith. It's about the profound journey of self-discovery and embracing one's true purpose. This alignment brings a sense of fulfillment that surpasses all understanding, a joy from knowing you're on the right path, even when the destination is unknown.

By sharing our stories, we light a path for others, offering hope and inspiration when the way seems dark. We demonstrate through our lives that it's possible to rise above fears, overcome doubts, and build a life that reflects our highest ideals and aspirations.

As I move forward, I commit to living as an example of what's possible when you dare to listen to your heart and follow its guidance. It's about embodying the principles of faith, courage, and perseverance in the face of uncertainty. This commitment isn't just for me but also for others who may find encouragement in my story and see my journey as a reflection of their potential and possibilities.

Looking ahead, the vision is clear: a world where each individual is encouraged to discover and pursue their unique purpose, supported by a community that values diversity, embraces change, and champions courage. To realize this vision, we must continue to share our stories, reach out in mentorship, and build bridges of understanding and support.

KELLI HUDSON-KEY

About Kelli Hudson-Key: Kelli Hudson-Key has built a remarkable career that speaks volumes of her dedication, leadership, and passion. Currently, she holds the esteemed position of Senior Division Executive at Park Lane Jewelry. In this role, she plays an instrumental part in the company's growth and success, leading her team with a unique blend of wisdom and enthusiasm.

Before her tenure at Park Lane Jewelry, Kelli showcased her prowess in the realm of direct sales with Mary Kay Inc., a global powerhouse known for its impressive legacy spanning 60 years in the beauty industry. For over 22 years, she contributed significantly to the brand as Senior Sales Director. During this time, Kelli was integral in fostering the company's sales strategies, solidifying its position as one of the leading direct sellers of personal beauty products in the United States.

Her longevity and success in the industry is a testament to Kelli's unparalleled drive and commitment. Her knack for understanding market dynamics, combined with her talent for nurturing and guiding her teams, has marked her as a leading figure in the direct sales sector. In every endeavor, Kelli Hudson-Key's name is synonymous with excellence, leadership, and an unwavering commitment to success around the world.

Message me at: *m.me/Kelli.HudsonKey*

Author's Website: *www.MyParkLane.com/KelliKey*

Book Series Website: *www.TheBookOfMentors.com*

LAUREN COBB

A JOURNEY OF MOTHERHOOD, RESILIENCE, & PERSONAL GROWTH

Navigating Life's Challenges

As I reflect on my journey through life, it's clear that it's been a rollercoaster of ups and downs, much like the experiences of many others. Yet, I've been blessed with a mostly positive attitude, which has helped me weather even the toughest storms. However, when faced with the challenges of pregnancy, that optimism was put to the ultimate test.

Our journey into parenthood began smoothly enough with our first baby. Despite the usual pregnancy experiences, such as the adjustment period and delivery, it was a relatively easy transition into motherhood. Life seemed to fall back into place seamlessly, allowing us to continue traveling, enjoying ourselves, and maintaining a healthy lifestyle.

When I shockingly became pregnant again, the experience was physically grueling. I was constantly plagued by sickness, rendering me unable to care for our three-year-old daughter without assistance. Despite the challenges, we persevered, and our baby girl arrived a little earlier than expected, but healthy and robust, weighing in at 8lbs 4 ounces.

Unfortunately, my body struggled to recover from the demanding pregnancy, and our newborn presented additional challenges. Sleepless nights, weight gain issues, and a general sense of unease plagued those early months. With my husband completing his final year of college and limited support from family and friends, I found myself overwhelmed and hesitant to admit that I was struggling to cope.

Just as we began to find our footing, life threw us another curveball—an unexpected third pregnancy. I was shocked and initially in denial, especially considering our second child was only a year and a half old. However, this pregnancy was unlike anything I had experienced before. From the very onset, I was beset by extreme morning sickness, diagnosed as Hyperemesis Gravidarum, which required frequent hospital visits and extensive medical intervention.

Despite the outpouring of support from friends and family, including my incredible sister who stepped in to care for my daughters while I battled through the difficulties of pregnancy, I found myself sinking into a dark and despondent state. The physical toll of the illness combined with the emotional strain of managing two young children took its toll, leading to moments of despair and questioning.

I vividly remember one night, lying in bed, tears streaming down my face, grappling with intrusive thoughts of whether it would be better if I weren't pregnant anymore. The sheer terror of such ideations shook me to my core, leaving me questioning my worthiness as a mother and the viability of my unborn child. It was a harrowing period, culminating in postpartum depression following the birth of my third daughter.

For two years, I battled silently, attempting to mask my struggles beneath a facade of normalcy. Yet, the loneliness and despair persisted until I finally sought professional help. The day I poured my thoughts onto paper in the doctor's office marked a turning point, a pivotal moment of acknowledgment and acceptance. With medication and therapy, the clouds began to part, albeit slowly.

However, it wasn't until I embraced the power of autosuggestion and paradigm shifting that true transformation occurred. Reconnecting with myself, I utilized daily affirmations and visualization techniques to rewire my thought patterns, fostering a renewed sense of hope and agency. Drawing inspiration from mentors like Bob Proctor and Napoleon Hill, I recognized the importance of cultivating a positive mindset and aligning my actions with my aspirations.

Through diligent practice and unwavering faith, I gradually emerged from the depths of despair, reclaiming my identity and reigniting my passion for life. Armed with newfound clarity and purpose, I embarked on a journey of self-discovery and personal growth, leveraging the principles of autosuggestion to manifest my dreams and aspirations.

Today, as I stand on the precipice of possibility, I am filled with excitement and anticipation for the adventures that lie ahead. With my husband by my side, we are committed to realizing our shared dreams, from exploring the Amalfi Coast to savoring homemade pesto in Cinque Terre. Together, we are rewriting our narrative, one paradigm shift at a time, embracing the boundless potential of the human spirit.

In closing, I urge you to embrace the power of autosuggestion and faith, for within lies the key to unlocking your fullest potential. As you embark on your own journey of self-discovery, remember that every challenge is an opportunity for growth, and every setback is a steppingstone to success.

Dare to dream, dare to believe, and dare to create the life you've always envisioned. The possibilities are endless when you harness the power of your mind and align your actions with your deepest desires.

LAUREN COBB

About Lauren Cobb: Lauren Cobb is a wife to her amazing and supportive husband Tyler. A mother to 3 beautiful daughters who've taught her more in the last 12 years than she has learned in the first 23 years of her life.

At a young age Lauren knew she had a lot of ambition and drive. As she became an adult, she knew that entrepreneurship was her passion and thankfully married someone who supported that! Together with Ty they own a graphic and media design company that they've built from the ground up. Growing and seeing the successes from their own efforts has been one of the most rewarding experiences!

Self-development and leadership have been a big part of Lauren's life since she was 14. She traveled and taught leadership to youth across the country throughout her high school years. She knows first-hand how self-development is crucial to success in life. Knowing who you are and finding your purpose and passion is important.

As Lauren and her husband Ty are building their businesses and seeking a network and friends who are aligned with their values, they've found in Champion Circle and learned how to properly mastermind. Lauren is a member of the corporate executive team at Champion Circle Networking Association, founded and led by Jon Kovach Jr. Masterminds have changed her life and their business for the better.

Author's Website: *www.TyCobb.MyPortfolio.com*

Book Series Website: *www.TheBookOfMentors.com*

LIZ SEARS

HOW TO ENGAGE WITH YOUR MENTOR

Have you ever noticed that life can change in an instant? You can hear something you've heard many times before, but this time it resonates with you in a new way. You can feel in your core that life just shifted.

Have you also noticed that when something profound occurs in your life, you remember the most inconsequential details? I had a moment like this. I was cleaning the kitchen and listening to an old recording of Bob Proctor that someone had uploaded to YouTube. He started talking about how if you want to change your life, you need to get crystal clear about who you want to become. You need to get a detailed picture of what that person's life looks like and how they show up to create that life.

What do they say?

What do they do?

Who are their friends?

How do they plan?

How do they execute their plans?

What do they read?

And so on.

And then you behave like that now. You become that person now. You talk like them. You act like them. You plan and execute like them—and as a result, your life will build around it.

I paused both the video and what I was doing and stood there stunned. He was right! I'd heard that before but realized I hadn't become that person. Instantly, I recalled a comparison I'd heard Tony Robbins make that taught the same lesson. Tony said that how you view yourself impacts your decisions, and he shared an example about a man who decides to quit smoking.

Scenario #1: Someone offers this man a cigarette, and the man replies, "No thanks, I'm trying to quit."

Scenario #2: Someone offers this man a cigarette, and the man replies, "No thanks, I don't smoke."

You can hear the distinct difference. When it clicked in my brain about becoming that person, I was standing on the left side of the island in my kitchen drying my green mixing bowl. Yup, I was remembering inconsequential details. But that's how I knew it was one of "those" moments.

So, I grabbed my journal, went to the couch, and considered the woman I wanted to become. I began to write. I filled a full page outlining what her life will look like on December 31st this year. Then I filled two pages on how she shows up to create that. During the entire exercise, the room was brighter, I could see the words more clearly on the page, and my mind felt physically expanded.

It was weird and amazing!

But what was most awesome about this experience is that it wasn't an isolated experience. I've had several large moments like this and hundreds of smaller ones because I seek them out. I share how to choose your mentors in the first book of this *Book of Mentors* series, and in this book, I will share 3 ways to best engage with your mentors.

#1: Expect a Golden Nugget

Whether listening to a recording or verbally talking to a live person, the first key to engaging with your mentor is to expect to hear a golden nugget. Expect that something they say will trigger a clear recognition of an area for growth.

Another tip is to enter the conversation with the thought, "How open-minded am I?" This approach can remove the barriers that prevent us from learning. It's wise not to believe everything you're told. However, it is wise to consider what you're told, use critical thinking, and glean what benefits you.

Lastly, embrace the perspective that "I know what I know, but I don't know what you know." Listen, ask questions, and use this opportunity to learn. It's often easy to hear someone begin speaking about something you're familiar with and then tune out what they're saying as your thoughts take over. But as we listen for nuances that differ from ours, we can generate great coaching and mentoring conversations.

#2: Identify Your Intention

My family had chickens growing up. And sometimes we had to catch the chickens and put them in the hen house. If I entered the chicken run and tried to catch any chicken close to me, they all seemed elusive, and it took much longer. But if I went in and decided which one I would catch first, catching them all took less time and was more effective. This is how it can be with learning. If we go in and just listen to whatever comes up, most likely none of the information will make a significant difference in helping us improve our lives. A clear mental picture of what you want to learn next will focus your attention and help you recognize the golden nugget that will move your life forward.

Several years ago, I chose to learn all I could to become better at delegation. It was fascinating to read the books and discuss with my mentor and coach how to delegate better because although I'd heard much of this before, subtle distinctions were landing differently with me. I recognized small adjustments I could make that would create large results. Then in a coaching call, I shared with her what I'd been doing, but because I failed to communicate that "my intention" was to share "a win" with her, she was listening with the intention to coach me!

At the end of my story, she started asking questions to help me discover where I could improve and instead of feeling awesome, I felt frustrated. I didn't realize that I didn't want coaching at that moment and, instead, I just wanted to share how I was implementing what I'd learned.

Luckily, from my answers to her questions, she recognized what happened and called me out on it: I was on a coaching call, after all, and failed to be clear on my intention which set us both up for failure. What a great learning experience! It caused me to become more aware of the times when someone I mentor and coach speaks with me and may just have the intention of sharing a "win." Clarity of intentions makes a difference!

#3: Take the Coaching

It's common for people to view their limiting beliefs as who they are. People will say things like:

I'm bad with names or

That's just how I am or

I'm overwhelmed or

I could never earn more than $

Wording beliefs as though they're facts makes it difficult to overcome them. Consequently, when we view limiting beliefs this way, we take them on as our identity and view any attack on the belief as a personal attack. I've heard people defend limiting beliefs with absolute conviction that that's who they are. "Take the Coaching" means that when we learn something that challenges or disproves our limiting belief, we step out of the identity of that belief and examine it with the mentor. "Take the Coaching" means we get on the same side of the negotiation table with our mentor and look across the table at the belief and get curious. We dissect it: Where did it stem from? How does it show up in our lives? How might it be holding us back?

"Overwhelm" was a very powerful limiting belief that my coach helped me to overcome. The first (and only) time I said to my mentor, "I'm feeling overwhelmed," she had me spend 5 minutes looking for it! I had to look under the desk, on the bookshelf, under the chairs, on the wall, and on and on. I kept saying, "Okay, I get it." But she didn't let up until it was crystal clear that overwhelm doesn't exist except inside my head as a belief. The amazing thing about beliefs is that because they exist solely inside our minds, we can change any of our beliefs instantly to something else that serves us better.

Whoa. This was one of "those" moments for me. So, you can imagine how fun it was the next time when I shared with her how I was negotiating a business transaction that felt less than fair, and my coach said, "Alright Liz, stand up. I want you to look around the room and find 'fair.' Look under the desk..." Okay. I get it. Fair doesn't exist, either, except inside my head.

Since "fair" doesn't exist, it boils down to whether or not something works for me. If it doesn't work, then it's my responsibility to communicate and renegotiate. And that's really what this is all about. If something in my life isn't what I want or isn't what I'm striving for, then it's not only my responsibility to do something about it, it's also my right. And if there is anything in your life that you want to be better or it isn't working for you, mentors are a beautiful way to help you break into the next amazing version of you!

LIZ SEARS

About Liz Sears: Liz Sears lives her life in every way to fulfill her life mission which is to "inspire the masses to live lives full of connection, contribution, adventure, and impact" As a speaker and writer, she focuses on the consistency of striving towards becoming the best version of ourselves and sharing how to be awake and engaged in life. She fully believes that life, with its extensive variety of obstacles and opportunities, can be an amazing adventure. It's all about how we play the hand we were dealt and what we choose to create.

Liz has been married to her best friend since 1996 and together they have raised four wonderful sons. She is a proud alumna of Kent-Meridian High School and pursued Business Administration/Management at the University of Utah. Her roots trace back to Seattle Washington, but she and her family now call Layton, Utah home.

Beginning in the financial industry in 1995, Liz's career path has included roles such as Mortgage Loan officer, Property Manager, Real Estate Investor, and most recently as Team Leader and Associate Broker of Utah's Elite | REALTORS® at Real Brokers, LLC. She has served many times in leadership roles in the Real Estate industry including on the Board of Directors for the Northern Wasatch Association of Realtors and as a Governing Board Member of the Women's Council of Realtors Utah.

Author's Website: *www.UtahsEliteRealtors.com*

Book Series Website: *www.TheBookOfMentors.com*

M. A. FULTS

MENTORING LEGACIES

. . . .

"I am a spiritual person living in a human body,
not a human body with a spirit."
~ Bob Proctor

For this *Book of Mentors* series, each Volume has a tag line of "Honoring Legacy Legend…" And, I propose, each volume and each chapter therein is its own legacy—a Legacy Stone, if you will. A Stone along the path of whoever picks it up to read. A Stone that can be 'stepped' on multiple times. A Stone extending the Legacy of each honored mentor. It is an honor and a privilege to provide my own stone to the pathway.

"Change is constant and inevitable, but personal growth is a choice."
~ Bob Proctor

Personal Growth

Years ago, after joining my third ship, USNS WACCAMAW (T-AO 109), I was chatting with new friends and one of them mentioned Jimmy Buffett…my response was, "Jimmy who?" Needless to say, I was castigated, vilified, and made to feel a complete idiot. I didn't know who Jimmy Buffett was?!? Ah, the shame. I then endured at least 15 minutes of on-the-spot education in all things Jimmy Buffett, leading off with "Margaritaville" (a song which I HAD heard, just didn't know the singer).

In my defense, I'd spent most of my life either in foreign countries with my Army father, attending the University of Arizona Drama Department, or stationed on the West Coast where Buffett was not quite as big as on the East Coast. And therein 'lies the rub,' to quote Shakespeare—which I can do quite well, thank you. I was never exposed to Buffett, beyond hearing a song or two, and so was ignorant of who he actually was. My new friends were all from the eastern states, had been listening to him for years, loving his music, words, sentiments, and some possibly saw Jimmy Buffett as a mentor. Which leads me to, who were MY mentors through the years?

In the last Book of Mentors, I shared two mentors in my life who helped me to learn, to grow, to become a better leader. But my question to myself remains: Who had I chosen to mentor me?

"A mentor is someone who sees more talent and ability within you, than you see in yourself, and helps bring it out of you."
~ Bob Proctor

Note: While mentors may see and bring out of us that which we don't see in ourselves, we choose those we want to follow. We chose the men and women who present a path leading toward the goals or results we desire. And most often, there is more than one mentor, even during the same season in our lives.

So, I asked myself, if my response to hearing the names of the men being honored in this series was, "___ who?" then where had I received the knowledge, prompting, kick-in-the-pants, and growth which so many others found through the words and wisdom of Zig Ziglar, Bob Proctor, Dr. Wayne Dyer, and Jim Rohn?

Second note: I have found myself blessed through not only researching each of these great mentors, but also through hearing or reading how others have found and been blessed by their words, their mentorship. This includes my current pastor, friends, and even within books I've recently read.

The answer to my question was not one person. It was not one line of focus, drama, philosophy, religion, or specific field of study. It was not any one thing, it was a combination of many things. I was mentored through books I read, of drama, history and philosophy, human frailty and heroics. It was movies and television shows, comedy and tragedy, psychology and education. It was songs of love and pain, music of emotion and mathematical precision.

I found my mentors to be from all walks of life, all backgrounds and beliefs. And I still find these mentors, who have shared their thoughts, beliefs, and revelations with me, through words, music, and actions. If you'll permit me, I'd like to share with you, dear reader, just some of the vast number of "Legacy Stones" I have found in books over the years.

Confession: I am a slow reader. I read every word, even though I've been told not to, in order to read faster. But I love, with a capital L, to read stories, ever since I was 'forced' to go to remedial reading the summer between 2nd and 3rd grade. I can still remember the home and the collie, named Bella, who always greeted me. That summer my tutor ignited in me an excitement and a hunger for reading. I discovered that I could go anywhere in the pages of a book, and my knowledge, my wisdom, my abilities grew with each book I devoured. Even if it took me longer, I would read through to the end, and then head back to the library for the next book.

Yes, in those early years I read Nancy Drew and the Hardy Boys, the Happy Hollister's, and, two books that were so special to me: One, "An Otter's Story" by Emil E. Liers, and two, Ester Wier's first book for children and young adults, *The Loner*. This book about a young lonely boy, finding a home and courage with an elderly, equally lonely frontier women, touched my own lonely heart, which is why I still remember that book fifty five years later.

One other book of note I read during those early years, a book about George Armstrong Custer, "youngest general in the Civil War," "hero" of the West. It took me a long time to 'forgive' Custer, after I read *Bury My Heart at Wounded Knee*. Feeling betrayed by him, I developed an unhealthy hatred. When I realized he was long dead, didn't deserve my holding onto a hatred for him, AND I was only poisoning myself, I let the hatred go—one of those pathways better abandoned than followed.

The legacy stones from the beginning brought me adventure and a desire to solve problems and mysteries. The authors gave me a sense of life greater than the small world I inhabited, of possibilities that were in essence endless. And they gave me a courage and a confidence that I, too, could go out and boldly meet whatever lay before me.

Into middle and high school, other authors were added, like Zane Grey and Louis L'Amour. Westerns were easy and often, even for me, quick reads. But Louis L'Amour was special amongst the many other writers of Western fiction. He wrote of the Sacketts traveling west from the Smokey Mountains to San Francisco. He wrote of heroes and heroines who used their brains before brawn, their strength, their determination and their faith. And I absorbed every single book I could get my hands on.

I also found James Michener and James Clavell, traveling through Europe with "The Drifters," and feudal Japan with "Shogun," respectfully. And I found Alastair MacLean, who took me on adventures behind enemy lines, scaled cliffs to destroy mighty guns, took the 3:10 train to Yuma, and waxed philosophical while hiding in a basement.

These legacy stones led me to paths of my own adventures culminating in joining the US Navy. The paths were challenging, requiring courage and self-confidence, but my personal growth continued, and my belief in myself, my abilities, my future, also increased.

While at University, my Aunt Muriel led me to an author who became one of my favorites, Anne McCaffrey. McCaffrey's *Restoree* was a science-fiction book that captured my attention and opened up another world for my book-loving mind. And most importantly, most of McCaffrey's books had women, young and old, who led teams, found solutions, never quit, pushing through adversity, major disasters, loves lost and lovers found. They never saw or believed that being a woman limited them. Her Dragonriders of Pern series is still one of my all-time favorites.

With this new found discovery of science-fiction, I was soon reading Piers Anthony, one of the most prolific sci-fi authors (if you love puns, his Xanth series is a must read); Isaac Asimov; L. Frank Baum; Ray Bradbury; Frank Herbert; Stephen R. Donaldson; and David Eddings. I fell in love with the genre because of how far I could go, "To infinity and beyond."

I will be forever grateful to my Auntie M, as "Restoree" was a legacy stone which led to the opening of my imagination and to my confidence as a woman. The path of possibilities within science-fiction was so exciting, so invigorating, I came to believe that I can do anything I set my mind to, and my imaginative mind was brimming over.

I leave you with this last Bob Proctor quote:

"Faith and fear both demand you believe in something you cannot see. You choose!"

I've learned to choose my mentors wisely, noting the legacy stones on the path, and most importantly the direction the pathway leads. Not all paths are meant for me, not all paths are meant to be traveled my entire life. I choose those which bring me love, joy and peace…those are the ones to remember, and maybe even to walk on again, when I need more love, more joy, and more peace in my life.

M. A. FULTS

About M. A. (MaryAlice) Fults: Born into an Army family, and with 39 years serving in and then working for the US Navy, means Fults spent many years traveling and living in foreign countries including four years in Teheran, Iran. She has a BFA in Drama Production from the University of AZ and a MS in Management from Naval Postgraduate School in Monterey, CA. After retiring for the second time in 2022, Fults continued her life-long pursuit of learning, while embarking on her new found passion of Heart Healing, Financial Advising and Life-Coaching. She has been blessed with one son.

Book Series Website: *www.TheBookofMentors.com*

*"MONEY IS ONLY USED
FOR TWO THINGS.
ONE, IT'S TO MAKE
YOU COMFORTABLE.
THE OTHER IS THAT
YOU CAN EXTEND THE
SERVICE YOU
PROVIDE FAR BEYOND
YOUR OWN
PRESENCE."*

~ BOB PROCTOR

MARIS SEGAL & KEN ASHBY

THE INSOMNIAC LAW OF ATTRACTION

We have one life to live, one body, and one planet and all are simultaneously seeking our attention. As we navigate life seven days a week at work, home and beyond, 24/7 we are in relationship with someone or something including ourselves from the time we awake through our sleep and dream state. We call this relationship immersion, The RFactor. It is our relationship with ourselves consciously and subconsciously that shapes our desired dreams and impacts our intentions, choices, actions, and ultimately, accomplishments and results in our personal and professional lives.

This is where the masterful Godfather of personal development, Bob Proctor, comes in. He certainly transformed our lives as individuals and as a thriving couplepreneur. With Bob Proctor's wise leadership, teachings, books, programs and his contribution to the iconic film, *The Secret*, he mentored millions of us globally to live in the clarity of "The Law of Attraction."

Central to Proctor's teachings is that "like-attracts-like" and that thoughts have the power to manifest reality. His words are constant, "The Law of Attraction is always working and never sleeps!" Let's be real, this 24/7 law of attraction must be a law for insomniacs in the pursuit of attracting their desires and breathing them into reality, and that could be every human on the planet. His interpretation of this universal law emphasizes the importance of thoughts, feelings, actions, and results in achieving our desires large and small.

For us, Proctor's wisdom has also been his constant authority that "we attract what we focus on" (positive or negative) and that our reality in our external world reflects our inner mental mindset and emotional state. Thoughts and feelings have a direct impact on reality, attracting positive or negative experiences into our life. It runs on the principle that like attracts like, meaning that positive thoughts and emotions will attract positive outcomes, while negative thoughts and emotions will attract more of what we don't want.

In short, the energy we put out is what people will resonate with and what will come back to us. We have a choice. Simple example, if you focus on not having enough money and what is lacking then your finances will keep taking a hit versus choosing to be curious and open to what is possible and seeing yourself in an abundant prospering place and building from there.

Positivity emits a different kind of energy that draws in more positivity. Easier said than done when we operate from our old patterns, we know, and it takes practice to build these skills and muscles. Trust us, we've been doing this work for many years with gratitude for its impact on us and others.

Think of the "Law of Attraction" like a persistent and nurturing house guest that won't leave, constantly whispering sweet affirmations into our ears at all hours. "Money flows to you with ease," "You are a magnet for success," "You will find your soul mate this year," it chants while we groggily stumble to the fridge for a midnight snack.

Bob Proctor guided us in the technique of actually seeing ourselves in the achievement and experiencing the feeling of our desires already fulfilled. As an example, someone seeking a life partner might declare, "I will find my soul mate by this date next year!" Then keep seeing and feeling it. Define all of the qualities that are important to you. See yourself in relationship with this person on the date you set. Visualize where you are, what you are wearing, how you feel, and what you are doing together. The more details, the better. Write it and declare it every day, share with your close circle, believe it, know it's already happened and live into it.

Stay true to your vision and the actions that support your commitment such as networking, dating, and meeting new people. Declarations only work when you do the work to realize them. Even on days of frustration, perhaps from a date that may not have been your favorite, know you can learn something from every experience and move forward. Truly the work is inside-out and how we are feeling about ourselves, what we tell ourselves shows up in our world relating with others. That's the energy and vibration that are very important in the "Law of Attraction."

"If you can see it in your mind, you can hold it in your hand."
~ Bob Proctor

As business strategists, coaches, and mentors in the Executive and Relational Leadership space, we work with our clients and their teams, ages twenty to seventy, on their human relations and interpersonal skills (AKA "soft skills"). This insomniac law supports our work as we harness its power to guide our clients in manifesting their vision and cultivating relationships in a culture of respect, responsibility reframing, and resilience. When vision and its clarity is shared collectively, whether in a family, in our community, among friends or at work, the results are astounding.

Maris: A few years ago, without one word written, we "declared" that we would become authors and have a Best-Selling Book and a TEDx talk within a year. Together, we wrote down our vision. We started writing, followed dead ends, participated in workshops, changed directions, connected with other writers and coaches, and, still, from all indications, we felt we were a long way off from manifesting our dreamy declaration.

Standing strong in our commitment, we shifted our frustration from "what was not working," to a positive visualization mindset approach of "what is working" and "what's possible." We went to a place of believing that it would be so and feeling our accomplishment in mind, body, and soul as if it had already occurred. Morning and night, we declared our vision aloud to each other like kids singing camp songs with sleepless repetition.

Then a few weeks later (seemingly out of nowhere), an opportunity door opened: we were invited to be featured co-authors in a powerful thirteen book series representing Napolean Hill's legendary book *Think and Grow Rich*. Thanks to the publishing team at Habitude Warrior, one year from the date that we began declaring our vision, we received notification that we in fact accomplished our author's dream. Soon after, we took our topic of Mastering Connected Relationships to the TEDx stage. None of this was by chance. We wrote it down with clarity, declared it daily with absolute belief, and visualized ourselves at book signings and as keynotes on stages! That was the proof and evidence that we needed to catapult our lives into a new stratosphere.

This sleepless law of attraction continuously responds to the vibrations we emit through our thoughts, emotions, and actions. We have experienced how it attracts into our lives opportunities that align with those vibrations and rhythms.

Ken: As a songwriter, on countless occasions, I have declared an intention to create a new song. I have been honored since my teens to have my work performed around the globe for millions from heads of households and classrooms to Heads of State. Feeling pressure to "get it right," I was often in my own way, leaving creativity behind versus leading with it. I learned to shift and be in play with the process. With no more than a hint of music and a few words scribbled on a napkin, I followed the flow to where it led, and allowed a new song to come through me.

This has happened more times than I can recall! From a world inside me, I visualize the lyrics, hear the music, and dance with an unwritten song as if it were already singing. When it comes to the creative process, which I believe is governed by the law of attraction, I never experience writers block because I know that the ideas will come if I remain in that zone, allowing my mind and body to "experience" a completed song. It is remarkable how when an idea surfaces it seems like a water tap has been turned on and complementing stories, supporting words, and musical form takes shape effortlessly when we don't let our negative mindset get in our way.

By consciously choosing to focus on positive thoughts and empowering beliefs, we can shift our mindset and open ourselves up to new possibilities. Allowing the law of attraction encourages us to expand our awareness and embrace a mindset of abundance and possibility. By aligning our thoughts, beliefs, and actions, we can harness the power of the Law of Attraction to manifest our dreams and create the life we want.

As we honor Bob Proctor's contributions to the field of personal development, we have been personally inspired to embrace our own potential and create the lives we truly want by embodying the "law of attraction." The real "secret" is whether you are unaware of it, or whether you're shouting it from a rooftop, the Law of Attraction, as Bob Proctor told us, "Never sleeps" and there is no better slumber party around.

Whether we are awake or asleep, consciously aware or unaware, the Law of Attraction is at work, and we are its guide, manifesting our desires and beliefs. We continue to see how the importance of keeping a positive mindset and directing our focus towards what we truly desire is worth staying awake for.

We believe that yesterday's choices shape our present and today's choices determine our future!

> *"The law of attraction is always working, whether you believe it or understand it or not. Be like a postage stamp, stick to it until you get there."*
> ~ Bob Proctor

MARIS SEGAL & KEN ASHBY

About Maris Segal & Ken Ashby: Ken Ashby and Maris Segal, "America's Master Connectors," coach, consult, and collaborate with executives, entrepreneurs, celebrities and rising leaders to identify and bring their professional, personal, and philanthropic vision to life. Spanning four decades and forty countries, they combine their relationship marketing expertise with head and heart leadership to build meaningful connections and impactful strategies that drive their client's internal and external success.

Ken and Maris live by the philosophy that "We are all connected as human's first and that's where the bottom line begins."

Together and individually, working across the public and private sectors, they have served a wide spectrum of local and global leaders, consumer and financial brands, causes, and policy makers. This dynamic duo also leverages Ken's international award-winning singer songwriting gifts to develop collaborative teams with a songwriting workshop series. From board rooms and classrooms to Harvard, the White House, and Super Bowl Halftimes, Ken and Maris are also known for uniting diverse populations with innovative cross-cultural marketing and personal development programs.

As certified Executive and Relationship coaches, their latest book, *The RFactor; Universal Rhythms for Leading Prosperous Relationships* and their **DRIVE method:** **D**esire, **R**elationships, **I**ntention, **V**ision, and **E**mpowerment sit at the core of their work. Ashby and Segal set a path for every client to build high performing businesses and elevate personal and professional leadership for maximum impact and a 360-degree thriving life! As authors they have been featured in thirteen Amazon best-selling leadership centered books. They speak regularly and were recently featured on the TEDx Farmingdale stage.

Author's Website: *www.SegalLeadershipGlobal.com*

Book Series Website: *www.TheBookOfMentors.com*

MEL CARR

LEGACY EMBODIED: CLOVERSY'S TRIBUTE TO BOB PROCTOR

It's often said that we stand on the shoulders of giants, those who have carved paths before us, who have ignited our imagination and showed us what's possible. For me and my company, Cloversy, one such giant was Bob Proctor. His mentorship style didn't just impact my approach to business; it reshaped my entire perspective on ambition, growth, and service.

In this chapter, I want to share how Bob's legacy has woven itself into the fabric of Cloversy, an executive virtual assistant service designed to streamline the lives of busy professionals. It's a tale of applied wisdom and the enduring value of mentorship.

When I first encountered Bob Proctor's teachings, I was struck by his intelligent understanding of the human psyche and his unwavering belief in everyone's potential for greatness. His material wasn't just another self-help mantra; it was a call to alter your thought patterns fundamentally and approaches to problem-solving—something that is represented within the foundations of Cloversy.

The Paradigm Shift

'Paradigm shift' is a term Bob popularized, signifying a fundamental change in approach or underlying assumptions. At Cloversy, we consider the services of an executive virtual assistant not just as a commodity but as an indispensable innovation for successful entrepreneurs who juggle very active schedules and growing commitments. This paradigm shift, inspired by Bob's teachings, has encouraged us to prioritize strong and precise support systems that cater to the essential needs of our clients.

The Power of Visualization

Bob advocated for the power of visualization—mental imagery to manifest your desires. This technique became a staple exercise for our team, helping us envisage the successful execution of tasks and the satisfaction of our clients. By fostering this visual approach, we've developed a service identity that meets expectations and strives to exceed them, mirroring the profound value Bob saw in envisioning a richer, more fulfilled life.

The ABCs of Success

Bob's ABCs of success—Attitude, Belief, and Commitment—are principles we've instilled into Cloversy's company culture. Our attitude towards work echoes a professionalism that reflects Bob's own; our belief in the quality of our service is unwavering, and our commitment to our clients demonstrates the persistence Proctor encouraged. These guiding principles form the framework of Cloversy's promise to provide unparalleled executive virtual assistance.

Aiding Success in Others

Above all, Bob Proctor believed in aiding others in their quests for success. Our brand voice at Cloversy is proudly informative and persuasive because we recognize the profound benefits our services offer busy small business owners and professionals. Echoing Bob's mentorship style, we utilize clear, concise language coupled with testimonials that endorse the effectiveness and quality of our commitment to excellence on an executive level.

Every interaction with a client is an opportunity to impart a fraction of the mentorship I've discovered from Bob—an obligation to pay it forward. Therefore, Cloversy's focus has always been on the benefits that our executive virtual assistants bring to clients' lives, freeing precious time, reducing stress, and streamlining their business operations.

Testimonies of Impact

The impact of Bob Proctor's teachings is reflected in the successes of those we support. "Since working with Cloversy, I've reclaimed hours of my week," shares one of Cloversy's clients, a testament to how our services directly result in enhanced efficiency and productivity. Bob had always emphasized that the practical application of knowledge unlocks exponential personal and professional growth.

A Call to Excellence

We inspire our team and the readers, just as Bob has inspired us, to strive for continuous improvement and excellence. The call-to-action that drives our brand's messaging isn't merely a prompt for engagement but an invitation to experience the life-changing support that a Cloversy executive virtual assistant can offer. Through the culture of our services, clients learn to refine their delegation skills and learn to let go of those tasks that they should not be doing—a direct influence of the growth mindset Bob championed.

In conclusion, as this chapter illustrates, Bob Proctor's wisdom is weaved through the strategic, consultative, and supportive layers of Cloversy. His mentorship was a beacon that led me to craft a service centered around quality, improvement, and results. His ideas of personal development didn't just shape me; they became the cornerstones upon which Cloversy stands, unwavering and committed, in the service of today's active business owners.

The message I want to leave with you is that the most powerful legacy a mentor can impart is a living, breathing testimony through the actions and successes of their mentees. Through Cloversy, Bob's influence endures—a testament to the power of mentorship and the unforgettable impact of a remarkable individual.

And so, our tribute to Bob Proctor extends beyond mere words to the daily achievements of everyone touched by our service—it's a living, thriving embodiment of all that he taught and stood for. Here's to mentors like Bob, who lift us toward our highest aspirations and whose philosophies become more than ideas, transcending into actions that define our businesses and lives.

~ Mel C

MEL CARR

About Mel Carr: Mel Carr stands as a testament to the essence of profound introspection and self-awareness. She consistently dedicates time to understanding herself and those around her, seeking out beauty, meaning, and purpose in every facet of life. With an inherent ability to perceive what's "above and beyond" mere limitations, Mel's life resonates deeply with gratitude, humor, playfulness, and a graceful acceptance of the uncontrollable. Her innate curiosity allows her to unearth fresh and startling ideas, enabling her to engage wholeheartedly with life's mysteries and the sacred elements it holds.

As the esteemed Founder and Director of Cloversy, Mel possesses an uncanny understanding of time management and decision-making processes, irrespective of the content or environment. She's an emblem of organizational prowess, always at the forefront, ensuring every business need is met with precision and care. Mel's adeptness in resolving conflicts, enhancing brainstorming sessions, and fostering creativity sets her apart in the industry. She's ever attentive to customer feedback, ensuring prompt responses and resolutions to their queries. Infusing businesses with a fresh outlook and innovative ideas, Mel Carr is the catalyst that many organizations need to transcend their limitations. If you're looking to elevate your business, connecting with Mel is a promising pathway to boundless potential.

Author's Website: *www.Cloversy.com*

Book Series Website: *www.TheBookOfMentors.com*

DR. ONIKA SHIRLEY

I'M SO HAPPY & GRATEFUL I DECIDED

"Set a goal to achieve something that is so big, so exhilarating that it excites you and scares you at the same time."
~ **Bob Proctor**

I often tell myself that I don't have favorites. Although I tend to not have favorites, I have people and things I am certainly passionate about that I would choose over others any day. I think, while on this journey called life, it is vital to have individuals in which we value and that we understand. Bob Proctor was a virtual mentor to me, and I learned so much from him. One of his trademark sentences was, "Tell me what you want, and I'll show you how to get it." He read many books but one he read every day for years was, *Think and Grow Rich*. I read this book often and I also get a better insight every time I do.

It has been important to me to have great guidance from people who have successfully done what I am trying to do. I believe when we have good mentors it can give us great hope, fresh eyes, and open doors to new opportunities. We tend to minimize who we are, who we can become, and what we can accomplish. We hide our gifts and talents and believe that we can't accomplish what others have accomplished and tend to think more of others than we do of ourselves. Yet, the reality is we all have infinite potential. We all can dream big and reach our desired goals; however, we live within our "paradigms" and let them dictate what's possible for us.

Mentorship can help us manifest abundance while hitting our set targets, while living the lives of our dreams. When we work with a mentor, they help us to get in touch with our lost selves. Past experiences, traumas, and the lack of guidance can contribute to us not knowing who we really are, what we are capable of, and what we really want in life.

Those who truly want to improve their lives should have a mentor. I have learned over the years that the guidance of a good mentor will highlight that our successes and failures have absolutely nothing to do with how smart we are or where we came from, but it has everything to do with the multitude of habits we practice and live by day in and day out.

Although it doesn't have anything to do with how smart we are or where came from, it has everything to do with a station we have tuned into that has negatively impacted our subconscious mind and is basically controlling what we think and what we do. Unless we change what, we're hearing "nothing's going to change."

You may ask how a person changes what they are hearing. A person can change what they're hearing by attending personal development events, listening to educational programs, and by using self-development products. You aren't limited to these; however, this is a great start, and these have helped me over the years. These things are sure to elevate a person's thoughts and successfully bring their personal best to the surface.

Having a mentor can be one of the greatest blessings a person can receive. Mentors help you think about things you may not think about on your own. Mentors can help you discover your purpose in life. Mentors help you build your self-confidence. Mentors can help you set goals, overcome fears, change your attitude, figure out the gap, and, most of all, change your beliefs.

How to Make the Most of Mentoring

To make the most of mentoring, you need to take initiative, be proactive, engaged, and accountable. I want to share seven things you can do to make the most of mentoring.

1. It is vital to set clear and reasonable expectations.

2. You need to have upfront boundaries with your mentor.

3. Communicate openly and honestly.

4. Be prepared for each session.

5. Listen attentively and be free of distractions.

6. Take good notes but make better notes of actions you're going to take.

7. Be ready to act on their guidance.

These seven things have made a world of difference as a mentee and a mentor. These have taught me to learn very practical techniques to feeling welcome, trusting my mentor to maintain confidences, while developing an action plan to enhance my overall performance. Having a mentor helps you to stay focused on personal improvement and life successes.

I have had several mentors but the one that took me to another level was the mentorship I received my Bob Proctor. Although I never had the opportunity to meet him in person, his teachings helped to determine what I wanted to accomplish, and his teaching made me think about what goals I wanted to set for myself and what targets I was aiming to hit. I decided. I decided that where I was is not where I wanted to be, and I decided to take action and to do something about it.

Bob would always say, "Two things you must know: Where are you now and where you want to go." These questions will cause you to be neutral and very honest with yourself and for yourself and once you understand you will see that your results are what you entitled to because they're what you're in harmony with. I know this is not something that you want to hear, and neither is it easy admit, but there's good news. You can get any results you want. I truly believe that we can get the results that we want; I believe in you just like I believed in myself. If you don't believe now, you can borrow my belief until you can develop it for yourself.

"What do you really want!?"

This is such a powerful and hopeful question. Time after time after time, I have thought about what I really wanted and what's so impactful to me is that I got it. I always get it. How, you might ask? I believed that I would. I would fantasize about what I really wanted while knowing that in my imagination there were not limits and neither were there any real barriers. As Bob Proctor would say, "Set your sights far above what is reasonable or practical, or probable."

Go after what is valuable to you. This is personal and it doesn't have to look like anything you have ever seen before. You can make it the way you need it be to get excited. You need to be excited enough to move yourself into action. If you're not in love with the idea, you will probably never turn it into anything worthwhile. Your love will start the process, and, depending on how deep you love it and how bad you want, it will keep you going. Some refer to this as your why. They say the why you started must really have meaning to you or you will quit before you really get started. Stop worrying about how and when it is going to happen and just believe that it is.

1. Dream and dream BIG.
2. Fall deep in love with the idea.
3. Make a commitment that you will do what needs to be done to live the life of your dreams.
4. Take the necessary actions.
5. Celebrate as if it has already happened.

The how will come and it will all happen by law. Right now, this may seem unreal but what you believe, you will receive. Change your beliefs and it can change your whole entire life. Are you ready to create lasting positive changes in your life? Can you imagine the life you've been dreaming about being your reality? Are you currently getting the results you truly want? Would you like to live a more fulfilling and abundant life? Would you love to be living in purpose?

If you answered yes to any of the questions above, take action, and connect with a mentor that could help you make it your reality and not just your dream. There's power in deciding and procrastination is a result of indecisiveness.

It's time to decide. What will you decide?

"The fear of making a decision is the result of fearing to make a mistake —the truth is, the fear of the mistakes has a greater impact on you than making the mistakes."
~ Bob Proctor

DR. ONIKA SHIRLEY

About Dr. Onika L. Shirley: Dr. Onika L. Shirley is the Founder and CEO of Action Speaks Volume, Inc. She is a Procrastination Strategist and Behavior Change Expert and known for building unshakable confidence; stopping procrastination, and getting your dreams out of your head into your life. She is a Master Storyteller, International Speaker, Serves in Global Ministry,

International Best-Selling Author, International Award Recipient, Serial Entrepreneur, and Global Philanthropist impacting lives in the USA, Africa, India, and Pakistan. Dr. O is a Motivational Speaker and Christian Counselor. Dr. Onika is the Founder and Director of Action Speaks Volume Orphanage Home and Sewing School in Telangana State, India, Founder and Director of Action Speaks Volume sewing school in Khanewal and Shankot, Pakistan. She founded, operated, and visited an Orphanage home in Tuni, India for four years and she supported widows in Tuni, India.

She is the founder of Empowering Eight Inner Circle, ASV C.A.R.E.S, ASV Next Level Living Program, and P6 Solutions and Consulting. She has served for 13 years as a therapeutic foster parent for the State of. Of all the things Dr. O does she is most proud of her profound faith in Christ and her opportunity to serve the body of Christ globally.

Author's Website: *www.ActionSpeaksVolumes.com*

Book Series Website: *www.TheBookOfMentors.com*

RITU CHOPRA

CONSCIOUS LEADERSHIP IN THE 21ST CENTURY

The legendary author and leader of our times, Bob Proctor, is known for his teachings on personal development and success principles, drawing heavily from mindset psychology and the Law of Attraction. His messages emphasize the power of thoughts, beliefs, and visualization in shaping one's reality. The essence of Bob Proctor's teachings can be summarized as he teaches that our thoughts and beliefs create our reality, and, by mastering our mindset, we can achieve our goals and dreams. Aligning our thoughts, feelings, and actions with our desired outcomes can attract success, abundance, and happiness into our lives.

Bob Proctor's principles revolve around empowering individuals to take control of their thoughts, beliefs, and actions to create the life they desire. He teaches that anyone can achieve success and fulfillment through mindset mastery, visualization, goal setting, and action.

We become what our beliefs and thoughts create our actions!

Conscious Leadership in the 21st Century

In our complex world today, as we navigate the dynamic landscape of the 21st Century, leadership has undergone a transformative shift from traditional hierarchical models to more inclusive and conscious approaches. Conscious leadership is not just a buzzword; it represents a fundamental evolution in how leaders perceive their role and impact on organizations and society. Here, we explore the core principles of conscious leadership in today's complex and interconnected modern era.

There are several principles and foundations that leadership for the next few decades of the 21st Century can be built upon. It's beyond personality type analysis, charts, graphs, or Enneagrams; it's heart centered.

The Foundations of Conscious Leadership

Conscious leadership goes beyond the conventional understanding of management and authority. It is rooted in a deep self-awareness that extends to a profound sense of the interconnectedness of people, systems, and the environment. Leaders who embrace conscious leadership are focused on more than just the bottom line; they recognize the importance of fostering a positive and sustainable organizational culture.

At it's core, conscious leadership involves mindfulness, authenticity, and empathy. Leaders who practice mindfulness are attuned to the present moment, enabling them to make more informed and thoughtful decisions. Authenticity involves being true to oneself and transparent in communication, fostering trust within the organization. Empathy, a cornerstone of conscious leadership, empowers leaders to grasp and connect with others' experiences, fostering a shared sense of purpose and unity.

Navigating Complexity for Success

The 21st Century's unprecedented complexity, marked by globalization, rapid technological advancements, and diverse workforces, requires a new breed of leaders. Conscious leaders excel in navigating this complexity by adopting a holistic perspective that considers the broader impact of decisions on various stakeholders.

Conscious leaders go beyond linear thinking, developing systems thinking to grasp the interconnectedness of elements within an organization. This enables them to address challenges at their roots, fostering sustainable solutions instead of reacting to symptoms.

Furthermore, conscious leaders promote ongoing learning and adaptability within their organizations. Recognizing the competitive advantage of learning and adapting in a swiftly changing world, they cultivate a continuous learning mindset. This approach empowers their teams to embrace change, experiment with new ideas, and perceive failures as opportunities for growth.

To achieve this, it is necessary to cultivate a supportive and inclusive culture where people feel valued, respected, and encouraged to contribute their unique talents.

Empowering & Developing People

Empowerment-focused leaders recognize the dual importance of a diverse workforce, both morally and strategically. Actively seeking varied perspectives, they acknowledge the creativity and innovation fostered by diverse backgrounds. Through inclusivity, conscious leaders equip their organizations to navigate global complexities. Beyond empowerment, these leaders are dedicated to continuous team development, investing in education, mentorship, and professional growth. This commitment enhances individual capabilities and fortifies the organization's resilience and adaptability.

Building a Purpose-Driven Culture

One of the hallmarks of conscious leadership is the emphasis on purpose beyond profit. In the 21st Century, organizations increasingly recognize the importance of aligning their activities with a broader purpose beyond financial success. Conscious leaders understand that a sense of purpose provides direction, meaning, and intrinsic motivation for individuals and the organization.

Conscious leaders cultivate a purpose-driven culture by articulating a compelling vision that transcends immediate goals. This vision inspires employees to contribute to a greater collective purpose. Under such leadership, organizations often prioritize social and environmental responsibility, positively impacting the communities they serve.

Conscious and charismatic leaders exude a magnetic quality, setting them apart and drawing people into their sphere of influence with an irresistible allure. This elusive charisma, challenging to articulate, plays a pivotal role in shaping the leader's capacity to inspire and mobilize others toward a common purpose. This exploration delves into the elements contributing to this unique charisma, analyzing its impact on communication, action inspiration, and cultivating a shared mission.

Balancing Profit & People

Conscious leadership dismisses the idea of a zero-sum game between profit and people. Instead, it pursues a harmonious balance, ensuring financial success without compromising the well-being of individuals or the broader community. This approach acknowledges the interdependence of sustainable profitability with the health, satisfaction, and ethical treatment of employees, customers, and the environment.

Moreover, Conscious leaders actively assess and oversee their organizations' influence on all stakeholders, understanding that enduring success relies on ethical business practices, social responsibility, and environmental sustainability. This dedication fosters trust and loyalty among employees, customers, and investors as financial goals align with a broader ethical framework.

Compelling Communication: The Art of Resonance

Conscious leaders are charismatic leaders. Charismatic leaders demonstrate mastery in communication, skillfully articulating ideas that deeply resonate with their audience. They possess a keen understanding of the emotional and intellectual needs of those they lead, tailoring their messages to elicit a strong response. This personalized approach leaves followers feeling seen, heard, and understood.

Infused with passion and conviction, the language used by charismatic leaders creates a contagious enthusiasm that sparks inspiration. Their communication transcends mere information delivery; it transforms into storytelling, vividly portraying a shared vision. Charismatic leaders engage the emotions of their audience through anecdotes, metaphors, and compelling narratives, rendering the mission both logical and profoundly meaningful.

Practicing Mindful Decision-Making

In our fast-paced and ever-evolving business landscape, decision-making is critical to leadership. Conscious leaders approach decision-making with mindful awareness, considering the potential consequences and ripple effects of their choices.

Mindful decision-making involves carefully considering both short-term and long-term implications for people, the planet, and other living beings. In mindfulness, leaders know their actions and take a rational, reflective approach to their decisions, considering values, purpose, and organizational impact.

Conscious leaders prioritize collaborative decision-making, valuing their teams' collective intelligence. They actively seek input from diverse perspectives, enhancing decision quality and fostering shared ownership and commitment among team members.

Decisions can be made in many ways, endured, persevered, and wavered. Visible conflict originates not only from opinions but also from rationale. Individuals have a multitude of decision-making avenues. It's possible to rely on instinct, consider multiple perspectives, analyze information, or ask others for guidance. Divergent perspectives on visible conflicts provide growth, understanding, and resolution opportunities. Being present to see, hear, and resolve issues at hand fosters healthy communication.

As we navigate the complexities of the 21st Century, foster purpose-driven cultures, empower and develop individuals, and balance profit with social responsibility, conscious leadership emerges as a beacon of guidance for leaders seeking to thrive in an ever-changing world. Grounded in mindfulness, authenticity, and empathy, conscious leadership transcends traditional models, emphasizing purpose, people, and ethical decision-making.

Conscious Leaders Have Charismatic Presence

At the core of a charismatic leader's aura is authenticity; it's the bedrock of charismatic presence. Authenticity engenders trust, and trust is the currency of effective leadership. Charismatic leaders are genuine and authentic, presenting a transparent and sincere persona to their followers. This authenticity creates a connection, as people are drawn to leaders who express their beliefs, values, and vulnerabilities with openness.

A charismatic leader's authenticity is not a calculated performance; instead, it emanates from a deep self-awareness and a genuine commitment to their vision. This authenticity is a foundation for the trust and rapport that charismatic leaders build with their followers, setting the stage for a compelling and influential leadership style.

Creating a Shared Mission: The Essence of Charismatic Leadership

Charismatic leadership's essence lies in inspiring and galvanizing individuals toward a shared mission. Leaders embody vision, passion, and authenticity, igniting followers' commitment. They cultivate trust and belief in the mission's significance through compelling communication and personal magnetism.

Charismatic leaders articulate a clear purpose, aligning it with followers' values, aspirations, and societal needs. They foster a sense of belonging and collective identity, empowering others to contribute meaningfully. Charismatic leaders mobilize diverse talents towards a common goal by infusing energy, optimism, and purpose, fostering collaboration, innovation, and resilience, thereby transcending individual agendas to create a shared sense of purpose and direction.

Engaging in Conscious Inquiry

Bringing unique perspectives to charismatic leadership involves exploring lesser-discussed aspects, challenging conventional wisdom, or integrating interdisciplinary insights. Here are some ideas to help you generate unique perspectives:

1. **Cultural Variations:** Explore how the perception and practice of charismatic leadership vary across different cultures. See how cultural values, norms, and historical contexts shape the manifestations of charisma and its effectiveness in leadership.

2. **Neuroscience and Psychology:** Delve into charisma's underlying psychological and neurological mechanisms. Consider how empathy, emotional intelligence, and authenticity contribute to charismatic leadership and how these traits can be cultivated or enhanced.

3. **Gender Dynamics:** Analyze how gender influences the perception and expression of charismatic leadership, whether there are differences in how charisma is perceived in male versus female leaders, and the potential implications for leadership effectiveness and advancement opportunities.

4. **Ethical Considerations:** The moral dilemmas associated with charismatic leadership, such as the potential for manipulation or exploitation of followers. Our responsibility is to examine how leaders can maintain ethical standards while harnessing the power of charisma to inspire and motivate others.

5. **Intersectionality:** Consider how race, ethnicity, socioeconomic status, and identity intersect with charisma and leadership. Leaders from marginalized or underrepresented backgrounds face unique challenges, and opportunities to leverage charisma effectively are apparent.

6. **Spirituality and Charisma:** Discover the role of spirituality, mindfulness, or personal development practices in cultivating charismatic leadership. Discuss how spiritual or contemplative practices can enhance a leader's ability to connect with others authentically and inspire meaningful change.

7. **Technological Influences:** Explore how technological advancements, such as social media and virtual communication platforms, have reshaped the dynamics of charismatic leadership. Discuss the opportunities and challenges of building charisma and influence in the digital age.

8. **Historical Perspectives:** Examine case studies of charismatic leaders from history, drawing lessons from their successes and failures.

Analyze how different periods' cultural and socio-political contexts influenced the emergence and impact of charismatic leadership.

9. **Follower Perspectives:** Consider the perspectives of followers and their role in shaping charismatic leadership dynamics. Discuss the factors contributing to followers' attraction to charismatic leaders and the potential consequences of blind allegiance or charismatic authority.

Conclusion

When we consciously inquire into our choices, we embark on self-discovery and self-awareness. This deliberate examination of our decisions allows us to explore the depths of our motives, values, and beliefs. It is a process of introspection that goes beyond the surface of actions and delves into the underlying layers of our consciousness.

Through this intentional reflection, we pave the way for alignment and authenticity. Alignment emerges as we connect with our innermost truths and align our choices with our core values. It involves a harmonious integration of our thoughts, intentions, and actions, creating a sense of coherence and purpose in our decision-making process.

In contrast, authenticity is cultivated from a genuine understanding of oneself. The art of expressing our values authentically and being true to ourselves is the art of being authentic. We can navigate our paths genuinely based on our desires and beliefs with the guidance of conscious inquiry, thereby shedding the pressures of societal expectations or external influences.

Through conscious inquiry, we unravel decision-making intricacies, deepening inner connection. This enriches life with purpose, empowering authentic choices and leading to fulfillment.

My personal experiences of decades of crossing paths with many scholars, leaders, and uplifted human beings has greatly influenced my consciousness journey to impact our shared humanity in positive ways!

RITU CHOPRA

About Ritu Chopra: Ritu Chopra, a technologist by profession, is an author, TV show host, award-winning film producer, a certified leadership coach, and an international speaker who is on her spiritual journey.

With 25+ years of experience in Fortune 500 companies serving in IT operations, information security in global financial, and healthcare industries, Ritu now mentors and coaches emerging leaders to achieve their 'Personal Mastery.'

She is Founder of Lead My Way, a Not-for-Profit Org, and a passionate advocate of Women Leadership and Empowerment Initiatives.

Author Website: *www.RituChopra.com*

Book Series Website: *www.TheBookOfMentors.com*

> *"ALWAYS ASK YOURSELF THE QUESTION, 'IS THIS GOING TO HELP ME GET TO MY GOAL OR NOT?"*
>
> ~ BOB PROCTOR

RUTHE HAGE

EMBRACING LIGHT ON THE MENTORSHIP JOURNEY

"A mentor is someone who sees more talent and ability within you, than you see in yourself, and helps bring it out of you."
~ **Bob Proctor**

As I reflect upon my journey, I am drawn to the profound impact that mentorship has had on my life. Mentorship, in its essence, is a beacon of light, guiding us through the tumultuous seas of life, and providing speed, support, and accountability. It is a relationship where someone believes in you, even when you are still learning to believe in yourself. They hold you high when you cannot do it on your own, and they reflect to you the potential and power that lies within, unleashing your limitless potential. This chapter is a tribute to the mentors who have illuminated my path and a reflection on how their guidance has shaped my journey.

Mentorship has the power to navigate, lead, and guide us through the complexities of life. It helps us develop greater faith in ourselves and in the world around us. It teaches us that everyone is loved, everyone is equal, and that it is our duty to give as much as we receive. This cycle of giving and receiving, of learning and teaching, is what mentorship is all about. It is a beautiful dance of growth, support, and transformation.

My first mentors were my parents. They were incredible students of life, constantly learning, growing, and leveling up. I was the child that was inquisitive and looked for answers and was willing to question an idea.

239

My parent instilled in me the faith and belief that everything is "figure-outable," and this foundation of resilience and resourcefulness has been invaluable throughout my life.

I soon realized that mentorship can come from anyone, anywhere, at any time. All it takes is an openness and willingness to receive. Some of the most profound lessons I've learned have come from unexpected sources, and I'm grateful for each person who has played a role in shaping who I am today.

As life unfolded, I found myself in the role of a wife and a mother, and then suddenly, everything turned upside down. My marriage ended, and I was left to navigate a dark and tumultuous time. It was during this period that I stumbled upon mentors like Bob Proctor. I reached out, took a leap of faith, and found myself being mentored. This experience was transformative, opening a world of possibilities and introducing me to a community of like-minded individuals. It taught me the importance of investing in myself, of paying for speed, knowledge, and accountability. Bob used to say, "Change is inevitable, personal growth is always a personal choice." It was a reminder that we are not meant to stay stuck and that there is so much more out there waiting for us if we are willing to reach out and grab it.

I had the opportunity to mentor with Bob Proctor in 2020 and then became one of his Proctor Gallagher Consultants. The shifts and awareness I gained being mentored have been transformative. Bob had a gift for taking a complex idea and simplifying it with his infamous "stick person." Understanding why we are stuck in old patterns, how we received them, and how we can replace them with a new idea is what Bob mentored so well.

Schools teach us knowledge, but not how to use our higher mental faculties from the source; our will, imagination, perception, intuition, reason, and memory. It is tapping into these higher mental faculties that give us the ability to create and transform. Bob was right when he said, "We are here from our creator to create" and "abundance is our birthright".

We are unable to change what we are not aware of. We are spiritual beings living a human experience in a physical body. And when this sinks in we can look at "our SELF" in a completely new and beautiful way. Creating a new idea, new thoughts and new inspired action is where the world around you will change.

We can create a new reality of ourselves which is our true identity before others told us differently. As we grow we evolve into a new elevated version of ourselves. Doing the work to release thoughts and ideas that no longer serve us and replace them with new thoughts and ideas takes the "kink out of the hose" and allows energy to flow to and through us. This raises our vibration and we then attract more of what we would love.

Looking back on that dark period in my life, I can now see that it was a turning point. It was a time of growth, self-discovery and fulfillment, and it taught me the importance of resilience, perseverance, and the power of community and faith. I am grateful for the lessons I learned and the person I have become because of them. I am grateful for taking that leap of faith and investing in myself. I encourage anyone who is feeling stuck or unsure to reach out and explore what's possible. You never know where it might lead you.

~ To infinite possibilities!

RUTHE HAGE

About Ruthe Hage: Ruthe Hage is a distinguished Mindset and Personal Development Coach, renowned for her ability to inspire and guide individuals toward unlocking their full potential and embracing their divine purpose. Based in Spring Creek, Nevada, Ruthe has dedicated her life to helping others illuminate their paths, drawing from her extensive experience and personal journey of transformation. Ruthe pursued a Bachelor of Education at the University of Nevada, Reno. Ruthe later transitioned into the financial world, where she worked closely with clients, helping them navigate their financial landscapes. Ruthe sought mentorship and guidance, finding it in the teachings of Brendon Burchard, Bob Proctor, and Sandy Gallagher.

Her experience being mentored by these influential figures was transformative, leading to profound shifts in all areas of her life. She has since become a Certified High-Performance Coach and Proctor Gallagher Consultant, dedicating her life to supporting others in their journeys towards personal and professional fulfillment.

Ruthe is the proud mother of three beautiful souls, a doting Nanna to two grandchildren, and blessed with two daughters-in-law. She is the founder of LUX Life Coaching, a platform through which she offers resources, support, and guidance to those seeking to brighten their lives and reach their fullest potential.

Author's Website: *www.msha.ke/RutheHage*

Book Series Website: *www.TheBookOfMentors.com*

SALLY WURR

WHAT TO LOOK FOR IN FINDING YOUR MENTOR

"Surround yourself with people who inspire you."
~ **Sally Wurr**

I appreciate the handful of mentors that I have been blessed to work with. They have shaped my life in ways that I would never have achieved on my own.

Not all people can fill this role. There are several traits a person must have in order to effect change in others. To best understand what to look for, you must first understand what a Mentor is. They can be a trusted advisor, a guide for a specific reason, and a supporter who can make a profound impact on your personal and professional growth.

We look for mentors for many different life situations. It could be that you are wanting to learn something new, like flyfishing. You would need to seek out someone that was an expert in that arena to help you out. Perhaps you are wanting to move up to the next level in your company— you may want to ask someone that has already had that position and ask them to help you develop the skills needed to do so.

I feel the most crucial aspect to consider when selecting a mentor is their expertise and experience in your desired area of interest. A mentor should understand the industry and have knowledge of all aspects of the role. Look for individuals who have a proven track record and possess the knowledge and insights you wish to acquire. Their experience can provide valuable guidance; in addition, they can help you avoid the common pitfalls and accelerate your progress.

Finding a mentor that you can work with needs to be built on trust, respect, and effective communication. You must feel a natural rapport and shared values for this alignment to create a foundation to work from. They must possess expertise and experience to be of help to you. A mentor who genuinely cares about your growth and is invested in your success will be more committed to supporting and challenging you to reach your full potential.

One of the first mentors I remember coming into my life was when I was in high school. His name was Mr. Glenn Newcomb, and he was my high school band director. I did not play a musical instrument in high school, but I was a majorette. I twirled my baton during high school football games, and we marched in parades all over California.

Between my Sophomore and Junior year of high school, he asked me to be the captain of the majorette squad, as well as the solo featured twirler. Just one of these roles would have been a feather in my cap! Being the captain of the majorette squad was a big deal at my high school. But so was the solo feature twirler spot.

During my Sophomore year of school, I was a member of the majorette squad. He was able to see firsthand how I handled myself with the other squad members, what I was able to contribute towards routines and teaching others what I knew.

It was because of his belief in me and my leadership skills that I was able to achieve both roles with much success in my Junior year of high school. You see, Mr. Newcomb was a great mentor and had exceptional people skills. He could find the key people he needed for each important role in the band. This allowed the band to win many awards for achievement.

He developed our leadership abilities by first stating that he believed in us. Whenever he found areas to help us excel, he let us know. In mentorship, it truly is "one for all and all for one." Everybody wins.

His greatest strength as a mentor was his willingness to invest time and energy in each of us. Mentoring requires a significant commitment of time and energy from all parties.

My second mentor was Mr. Skeeters. He was the owner and instructor of the Beauty College I attended. I was very fortunate that I was allowed to begin Beauty College in the summer between my Junior and Senior year of high school. During the school year, I attended two classes at my high school and my afternoons were in class at the beauty college.

Mr. Skeeters heard me make a statement that I was afraid of cutting people's hair. I was afraid, as I knew that once I cut someone's hair, I could not put it back on. This was terrifying for me, and he knew that. For the next two weeks, the only work I received was haircuts. He stood by me and coached me on how to achieve what the client requested. The more proficient I became, the less time he spent with me. I eventually became an expert hair cutter, and it was one of the favorite parts of being a Cosmetologist. As a side note, holding a Cosmetology license allowed me to be a hairstylist, nail technician, and esthetician.

Mr. Skeeters was a great mentor for me, as he possessed a delicate balance between offering support and providing effective feedback. You must look for someone who can provide honest assessments of your strengths and weaknesses while offering guidance on how to improve. A mentor who challenges you to step outside your comfort zone and provide actionable feedback fosters personal and professional growth. These types of mentors should be able to identify areas for improvement, encourage risk taking, and celebrate your successes. Mr. Skeeters did all of this for me.

Choosing the right mentor is a critical decision that can significantly impact your personal and professional development. You must consider the qualities and characteristics that you need from them. Their skills can help guide you on your journey to success.

Remember, finding a great mentor can help you with valuable support, help with guidance during challenging times, and inspire you to reach new heights. A great mentor will help unlock your true potential.

SALLY WURR

About Sally Wurr: Sally Wurr is an international speaker and multi-book author.

Sally is known as the "Storm Whisperer" because her message is about how to prepare for life's storms. Each person has trials and tragedies, but it is how we react to those events that help us grow and survive in our business and personal activities.

By sharing her expertise with stories, she teaches you how to embrace change and how to face life's struggles head-on. Simply put, she likes to teach others how to problem solve.

Sally embraces the knowledge that those who can must be the ones that do. She shares her stories so that others can find their true purpose.

In addition to writing and speaking, Sally is the President and Founder of SW Insurance Corp. She has helped thousands of CEOs develop employee benefits programs to attain and retain employees. It is her problem-solving and attention to detail that have made her successful in this arena for many years.

Author's Website: *www.SallyWurr.com*

Book Series Website: *www.TheBookOfMentors.com*

SARAH LEE

FORGET LUCK & REPEAT THE PROCESS

A reason I love this one is success leaves clues, and **success is not magic.**

Creating success is more like 1. knowing what you desire and want; 2. Learning how to do that thing; 3. becoming the person who can do it.

So often when we "manifest" something, we think manifestation means magic. It does not. There are a lot of "Sarah Principal" and "Sarah Lee Quotes," and one of them is around the idea that manifestation is just what right brain people call goals. Goal setting and business plans are for left brained people, but people who are right brained often relate better to the term "Manifestation" because they like the mystic implication; but the reality of it is, all of us create our lives.

We Create Our Lives with our Thoughts, Actions, & Habits

When we manifest something in business, it is because we believed in it so much and worked so hard (as well as meeting the 3 items above) that it creates a touch point for that thing to actually happen. I have never "created a circumstance," or a business that I did not first thing of obsessively and imagine in great, great detail, before even beginning to write it down, and put plans to it.

"All creation comes from desire, not from need."
~ Sarah Lee, MBA

When you want to learn to manifest or create your desires, you should learn to "enroll" people into your vision.

I did not say learn to sell, although you need to learn to do that too.

I said "Enroll."

I first studied enrollment from a wonderful coach named Marcia Weider. She was one of my coaches, had taught at Standford Business School, been a counselor to three U.S. Presidents, and also taught in her own Mystery School.

I always teach that mastering sales is just mastering a very effective and specific type of communication.

And where consultative sales, which is what Zig and Brian Tracy first invented, and from who I first learned about sales (besides from my Mom), is more about asking the right questions and understanding your prospect, your market, your product, and how to help the other person know how you solve their problem.

Enrollment is more like the communication that happens with influence.

Enrollment is more of using your words to connect with someone's values and value system and then asking them to take action.

Enrolling someone in your vision has to do with two or more parties and matched values, vs. in sales, communication is matching a problem with a solution.

Enrollment is something studied by Fundraisers, Nonprofit workers, Rotarians, Community Activists, Political Figures, Social Workers, Coaches, Speakers, and the like. People who value enrollment value a community of like-minded individuals and are willing to trade something to "be around or build relationships with powerful others," even if those others are not known or valued by all.

Enrollment is essential to building anything that gets big, that lasts, and has the power to move and/or affect a lot of people.

I, like many of you, studied politics at a deep level at university and working with Model UN, and I love the distinction.

Bob Proctor was a genius at enrollment as a speaker, influencer, and as a coach, and I appreciated watching him influence others, with his ability to enroll others into the way he saw life.

Bob, as many of you know, studied and read Think and Grow Rich almost every day of his life. He had some genius that many others did not, which was his desire to understand how to help himself achieve goals, combined with an ability to enroll others into his way of "seeing and being."

Another lovely example of someone I taught with in Clubhouse weekly for several years and am a best-selling co-author with, is Dame Doria Cordova. She is another lovely example of someone who has mastered the idea of enrollment. She never sells, she tells you what she believes, and listens for what you need and matches them up. Thus never selling a thing, but she is always naturally enrolling you to join in her and Bucky Fuller's mission work to help save the planet.

Understanding Hermetic Laws

I do not believe Bob Proctor invented as much as he discovered like a scientist.

We all act on the things we believe in, in life. That is a fact. Unless, and even if, you are very disciplined, your beliefs in life determine your actions. Beliefs determine what you will sacrifice for and what you will work towards. You will not manifest anything that you have not worked for or drawn to yourself through the use of your energy.

Since all of us are made up of energy, life is a level playing field in a way. That is why we are all born rich!

Understanding of how things work, and a little effort, and some minor resources, is all you need to create something in life.

So, why don't we believe and all know this?

My husband, Kerry, has worked with hundreds (often thousands) of other people, many he never even spoke to, to do visual effects at a Multi Academy Award Winning Level. They worked on movies like Titanic, Iron Man, Avengers, Thor, Harry Potter and Star Wars, to name just a few. I have had the privilege of watching his work come to reality, using "the hive mind," which is what we call it. All of the artists and actors combining into a single energy is how a movie gets made and communicated.

While working with Disney, the artists were all considered "cast members" and actors.

With visual effects, acting happens in the computer as much as it does with the actors' performances themselves. They often get little credit and not as much of the profits as some might think or hope, but they love the work, and that shows in how you, the viewer, come to perceive it.

Movies get made with enrollment. Without desire, enrollment, and a bunch of talented people, agreeing to be ego-less, and to work as one, we would never have some of the greatest entertainment we have ever seen to date. They know the ideas of success and teamwork, mostly from working and discovering them, but also, like all great teams, they practice what they know and BECOME that. They become the work itself.

All you see, hear, and think you know, is your reaction to energy, that's it. It's all we have here.

This is why understanding how to use energy, yours and others, to create something, is such an important part of the process to understand manifestation (read: creation).

I do not have enough time, or space (words) to get into this subject as deeply as I understand it.

But know this.

Time is relative. So is space. It is all only a perception.

One last thing.

All that ever existed, could exist, or will exists in some form or fashion now—you just have to learn to tune into it and match it with your own power and energy. Once you match it, completely, or as completely as possible, you will start to confuse the universe into testing to see if you meant what you focused on and if that is what you really meant and wanted, and if you can handle the responsibility of it, you will "get more;" and if not, you will still practice. That is one thing not well understood. The proof is in the practice, and while you practice, you are still contributing to the collective energy that feeds us all. Good or Bad.

This is why I always try to contribute positively to others, because you can only contribute or take when you are with people.

There are no neutral interactions in life.

I have used this idea of teaching people to walk on 1200-degree coals for Success Resources and the Tony Robbins organization, and the easiest way not to get burned is to repeat "I am one with the fire and the fire is one with me." Ironically, that is the same idea that George Lucas wanted people to understand with "the Force." This idea even ended up in one of the Star Wars movies, to my surprise.

You have to be "one with something" to use it to our advantage. As it is with all creation.

Once you tap into that, and believe it with all of your heart and being, you will understand Bob Proctor and his work. Bob could have been a physics professor, if he was educated and trained that way. What was once thought of as "New Age" is now understood as actual science, and that might be my favorite part of Bob's work. He brought physics to the masses in a way they could understand and use if they studied and understood its power.

And for that, Bob is not only one of the greats, but one of the icons of bringing the work of Napoleon Hill to life!

And for that, I will always love and admire him and it is an honor to help others understand a little bit more about him and his work.

SARAH LEE

About Sarah Lee, MBA: A brilliant educational psychologist and leadership expert by education, Sarah Lee is the innovative author of *Rock Soup - An Innovational Idea in Leadership.* By profession, Sarah has been teaching financial literacy for the last 15 years using her own firm as a platform. She is a full-service financial advisor and manager of her own Securities Branch of a national firm.

In addition, she networked with 100 Brokers all over the US. Sarah has an MBA in Finance and Social Impact and is 14 months shy of a Ph.D. in Educational Leadership. She is also the founder of multiple other companies and brands; some sold for profit, some she learned from, and some she consulted on other businesses. She is now mostly currently focused on her production company with her husband, MONEY MENTOR, LLC™.

She has been advocating and speaking on large issues like financial literacy, literacy, mindset, clean water, and service to the world (hunger, water issues, poverty, and literacy) for her entire life. She is the child of a public servant. Her father was a writer (he wrote textbooks on risk and insurance practices), a city councilman in a small town who taught Sarah civic duties, service to the public, and how the national political system works. She learned how to serve others, run a nonprofit volunteer group, and make a community impact. That led to an opportunity to be "on TV (not streaming) weekly as a host" as a nine-year-old. The opportunity became more interesting when they asked Sarah what she would like to produce for Kids-4 TV.

She said, "I would like to host a consumer reports show, where I would interview local business owners and see how I could highlight them while giving them ways to give back and make a difference." She was nine. That led to a life of public speaking, running endowments, and working with local universities on educational issues. She developed her world-famous business philosophy during this time: "Business is just like Rock Soup..."

Learn more about Sarah Lee, MBA, and follow her on FB: @coachmeSarahLee, @moneymentormethod; Instagram: @moneymentorcompany, @coachmeacademy. For Money Tips, you can text the words "MONEYMENTOR" to 55444 for a free gift or visit our webpage: *linktr.ee/MoneyMentorMethod*

Author's Website: *www.MoneyMentorFreeGift.com*

Book Series Website: *www.TheBookOfMentors.com*

STACEY HALL

EMBRACING CHANGE & GROWTH THROUGH POSITIVE MENTORSHIP

It's hard not to reflect on the profound shifts and the journey that has led me here. It's been a transformative period marked by challenges, personal growth, and an unwavering commitment to learning. As a dedicated dentist with a thriving practice, I have experienced firsthand how maintaining a positive mindset and surrounding myself with the right people can lead to remarkable personal and professional advancement.

In dentistry, every smile transformed is a testament to the dedication and skill of a dentist. A dentist's journey involves continuous learning, evolution, and compassion. Each patient interaction is an opportunity to provide care, uplift spirits, and instill confidence. The path to success in dentistry is paved with hard work, persistence, and a genuine desire to make a positive impact on the lives of others.

Navigating the complexities of oral health and well-being requires technical expertise and a deep sense of empathy and understanding. As a dentist, creating a welcoming and supportive environment for patients is just as crucial as mastering the latest techniques and technologies. Dentistry demands precision and kindness, and every procedure is an opportunity to make a difference in someone's life.

Through dedication and a passion for excellence, a dentist can truly make a lasting impact on the health and happiness of those they serve. A dentist's journey is not just about fixing teeth but about building relationships, fostering trust, and empowering individuals to smile brightly with confidence. As the world of dentistry continues to evolve, the commitment to growth, learning, and innovation remains at the heart of every successful practice.

The Power of Positive Thinking

Life, as I've learned, sometimes follows the path you plan. The past year brought its share of trials—navigating a divorce, managing a busy dental practice, and juggling motherhood responsibilities. Despite these challenges, I've found that embracing a positive mental attitude has been crucial. Influenced by thinkers like Bob Proctor, who teaches that "thoughts are things," I've realized our mindset's immense power over our circumstances. This philosophy has taught me that maintaining a frequency of positivity makes my world brighter and filled with possibilities instead of obstacles.

Despite the turbulence of the past year, I've come to appreciate the beauty in the unpredictability of life's journey. In those unexpected twists and turns, we find opportunities for growth and self-discovery. As I navigate the complexities of balancing personal challenges and professional responsibilities, I remind myself of the importance of resilience and optimism.

Drawing inspiration from the wisdom of mentors and Christ-like examples in my life, Bob Proctor shares his profound teachings on the transformative nature of thoughts. I've learned to harness the power of positivity in shaping my reality. Each day, I strive to cultivate a mindset that radiates optimism, turning hurdles into steppingstones and setbacks into lessons. Embracing this philosophy has not only shifted my perspective but has illuminated a path filled with endless possibilities and boundless potential.

Learning from Every Experience

Each hurdle has presented an opportunity for growth. During the most challenging times, including the complexities of a divorce, I chose to focus on learning and personal development rather than dwelling on the negatives. This mindset shift was not easy, but it was necessary. It allowed me to see that even amid turmoil, there is a chance to learn something valuable about oneself and life.

Through these difficult experiences, I discovered my inner strength and resilience. Instead of letting setbacks define me, I embraced them as lessons that would ultimately shape me into a better version of myself. As I navigated through the storms, I realized that challenges are not roadblocks but opportunities for personal growth and self-discovery.

With each hurdle overcome, I emerged stronger and more determined to face whatever life threw my way. The lessons I learned during those tough times became the foundation of my growth, helping me build a solid framework for a brighter and more empowered future. By embracing the opportunities for learning and development that challenges bring, I have transformed setbacks into openings toward a more fulfilling and enriched life.

Mentorship as a Catalyst for Growth

One of the most impactful aspects of my journey has been the role of mentorship. Maintaining my involvement in a specialized group of leaders called the Implant Study Club, an assembly of top dental professionals, has been a pivotal decision. This group meets bi-annually to share insights, successes, and failures. It's a unique forum where vulnerability is encouraged, and each meeting is a profound learning experience. Here, I've learned that growth often comes from unexpected places—not just from successes but from understanding and analyzing our failures.

The club's environment is built on mutual respect and the collective pursuit of excellence. We share a common goal: to enhance our skills and deepen our understanding of complex dental procedures. But beyond the clinical discussions, these gatherings are a source of personal support and encouragement, reminding me that professional growth is inextricably linked to personal connections and shared experiences.

The Implant Study Club has enriched my professional growth and fostered valuable personal connections. In this nurturing environment, I've come to appreciate the power of vulnerability and wisdom from sharing successes and failures with like-minded colleagues. Through our collective pursuit of excellence, we enhance our technical skills and strengthen our bonds, lifting each other up in moments of doubt and celebrating victories as a unified community. This club stands as a testament to the fact that true growth, both professionally and personally, flourishes in the fertile soil of supportive relationships and shared experiences.

Beyond the Classroom: Learning Through Connection

The traditional view of education emphasizes textbooks and structured courses, but I've discovered that some of the most significant learning occurs informally. Conversations with peers over dinner, discussing complex cases or new techniques, often provide deeper insights than formal lectures. These discussions allow for exploring ideas in a way that textbooks cannot replicate. They are dynamic, filled with real-world experiences, and tailored to the immediate interests and concerns of those involved.

Informal learning through engaging conversations has proven to be a valuable and enriching source of knowledge and growth. These discussions serve as a platform for sharing perspectives, challenging assumptions, and fostering creativity. The fluid exchange of ideas among peers encourages critical thinking and problem-solving skills in a context that resonates with real-life scenarios.

This interactive and personalized approach to learning enhances understanding and cultivates a sense of camaraderie and collaboration among participants. By embracing the power of informal learning, we open ourselves to a world of endless possibilities and insights that traditional education alone may not fully capture.

Family & Faith as Foundations of Strength

Amidst the whirlwind of professional responsibilities and personal challenges, my love for my daughters remains my deepest source of joy and motivation. Balancing life as a mother and a leader in the dental community has undoubtedly been demanding. Still, my unwavering faith and strong belief system have kept me grounded. These elements of my life provide comfort and guide me in making decisions that reflect my values and integrity.

My faith has been instrumental in maintaining my focus and resilience, encouraging me to approach each day with hope and a positive outlook. It's been my goal to embody these principles for my own well-being and to serve as a role model for my daughters, showing them that no matter the adversity, one can always choose to move forward in the best light, anchored by love and faith.

The Future Looks Bright

Looking ahead, I am excited about the future. My dental practice serves as my professional base and a platform for leadership and mentoring. While difficult, the past year's challenges have reinforced my commitment to mentoring and leading the dental community. I aim to inspire the next generation of dentists by sharing my knowledge and experiences, just as my mentors have done for me.

Through my practice, I also plan to continue my involvement in community service and outreach, extending the scope of my work beyond the confines of the clinic. These efforts are aligned with my personal values and my desire to make a positive impact on the world around me.

The past year's journey has been one of profound personal and professional growth. It has reinforced the importance of a positive mindset, the value of learning from every experience, and the transformative power of mentorship. As I continue to navigate the challenges and opportunities that lie ahead, I remain committed to the principles that have guided me thus far: optimism, perseverance, and the relentless pursuit of growth and excellence. Through these principles, I am confident that I can face whatever the future holds, armed with the knowledge that every challenge is an opportunity for growth.

STACEY HALL

About Dr. Stacey Hall: Dr. Stacey Hall, DDS brings her unique outlook on dental care and her personable optimism to the Williamsburg Center for Dental Health. After nine years of solid dental expertise as a dentist in Williamsburg, she then decided in early 2011 to branch out and open her own local practice, Williamsburg Center for Dental Health.

After completing her degrees from Virginia Tech in 1998, Dr. Hall graduated from VCU's MCV School of Dentistry in 2002, receiving her D.D.S. She is a member of the American Academy of Cosmetic Dentistry, Academy of General Dentistry, the American Dental Association, and was awarded member fellowship to the International Congress of Oral Implantology in 2008. Dr. Hall is a scholar with the internationally renowned Dawson Academy.

She is part-time faculty with the Academy, assistant teaching for courses concerning occlusion and rehabilitation of worn dentition. Dr. Hall also leads their ambassador program. Stacey has been blessed with three beautiful daughters, Lanie, Gracie, and Abbie, one attends school at the University of Tampa, and the other two are very active in high school. She is a loyal Virginia Tech Football fan and enjoys being on the water on her boat, relaxing at her river house, paddle boarding (even with her dog), skiing, Bible study, and missions work.

Author's Website: *www.WilliamsburgDentalHealth.com*

Book Series Website: *www.TheBookOfMentors.com*

> *"EVERYTHING HAS BEEN CREATED TWICE ONCE ON A MENTAL PLANE AND ONCE ON A PHYSICAL PLANE."*
>
> ~ BOB PROCTOR

STEPH SHINABERY

EMBRACING A MENTORSHIP REVOLUTION: AUTHENTIC ALIGNMENT

In today's rapidly evolving world, the traditional mentor-mentee relationship is transforming. No longer confined to hierarchical dynamics or one-sided knowledge transfers, modern mentorship is becoming a mutual journey of growth, discovery, and alignment. This evolution reflects a broader societal shift towards valuing authenticity, shared learning, and the creation of win-win situations for both mentors and mentees. Through the lens of my own experiences and the stories that have shaped my understanding of mentorship, I aim to explore this revolutionary movement and its potential to foster profound personal and professional development.

The essence of mentorship surpasses guidance and wisdom-sharing; it now embodies a dynamic exchange of perspectives, ideas, and experiences. In this paradigm shift, both mentors and mentees stand to gain valuable insights, fresh perspectives, and innovative solutions through collaborative learning and mutual empowerment.

In exploring the transformative power of mentorship, I have witnessed the profound impact of authentic connections, vulnerability, and empathy in nurturing growth and development. By embracing diversity, inclusivity, and open-mindedness, mentorship can break down barriers, challenge biases, and unlock untapped potential in individuals and organizations.

As we embrace this new era of mentorship as a shared voyage of self-discovery and mutual growth, we can co-create meaningful relationships, inspire positive change, and cultivate a community of support and encouragement.

The Essence of Modern Mentorship

At its core, mentorship in the modern context is defined by a deep, mutual connection that exceeds traditional boundaries. It's about recognizing potential, sharing wisdom, and nurturing growth to benefit both the mentor and the mentee. This perspective was vividly illustrated through my relationship with mentors like Steve (a mentor figure in my life), who, beyond providing professional guidance, invested time and energy into my personal growth. This depth of engagement highlights an essential aspect of modern mentorship: the willingness to share knowledge and oneself fully and authentically.

Having a mentor willing to go beyond just offering advice on career development can make a significant impact. Mentors like Steve are crucial in shaping our personal and professional lives. They share their expertise and provide valuable insights into life's challenges and opportunities.

The beauty of modern mentorship lies in the genuine connection between the mentor and the mentee. It's more than just passing on information; it's about building a relationship based on trust, respect, and understanding. Through this bond, both parties have the opportunity to learn and grow, gaining valuable perspectives and experiences along the way.

Having a mentor willing to share their knowledge, experiences, and even vulnerabilities can be a beacon of light. We can unlock our full potential through these meaningful connections and chart a course toward success and fulfillment. So, let us embrace the spirit of modern mentorship, where wisdom is shared, growth is nurtured, and relationships are cherished.

Alignment & the Win-Win Paradigm

Central to the evolution of mentorship is the concept of alignment—creating relationships based on shared values, goals, and visions for success. This alignment fosters a synergistic environment where both parties thrive, exemplifying the win-win paradigm. In my journey, moments of alignment with mentors have led to breakthroughs that were pivotal for my personal development and instrumental in achieving shared objectives. Such experiences underscore the importance of aligning mentorship practices with broader life goals, ensuring mentors and mentees find value and fulfillment in their collaboration.

The foundation of alignment goes beyond mere agreement—it's about establishing a deep connection rooted in mutual understanding and support. When mentors and mentees align their values and aspirations, the possibilities for growth and transformation are limitless. This harmonious relationship cultivates trust and empowerment, where insights flow freely, and challenges are tackled with resilience and creativity.

Reflecting on my own experiences, I am reminded of the profound impact that alignment with my mentors has had on shaping my journey. Within these moments of shared vision and purpose, I have discovered new perspectives, honed my skills, and dared to dream bigger than I ever thought possible. The beauty of alignment in mentorship lies in its ability to propel individual growth and catalyze collective success.

By embracing the power of alignment, mentors and mentees can co-create a dynamic partnership that transcends conventional boundaries. Together, they can navigate the complexities of personal and professional growth, celebrate achievements, and weather challenges with unwavering solidarity. In a world where connections are invaluable, fostering alignment in mentorship is not just a strategy—it's a transformative force that paves the way for boundless opportunities and meaningful relationships.

Living Authentically: The Ultimate Teaching

Perhaps the most revolutionary aspect of modern mentorship is the emphasis on living authentically. My mentors taught me that proper growth and fulfillment come from embracing our unique paths and speaking our truths, even when faced with adversity. This lesson, which I've come to view as the cornerstone of effective mentorship, encourages us to let our "divine light" shine, to be true to ourselves, and to impact others by sharing our authentic selves. It's a principle that guides my personal life and shapes my approach to mentoring others.

This approach to mentorship goes beyond just sharing knowledge and guidance; it's about fostering a supportive environment where individuals feel empowered to be their genuine selves. By leading by example and embodying authenticity, mentors can inspire their mentees to embrace their uniqueness, cultivate their strengths, and navigate challenges with resilience. This transformative process benefits the mentee and enriches the mentor by creating a more profound connection based on trust, respect, and shared experiences. Modern mentorship is a dynamic exchange that celebrates individuality, encourages personal growth, and cultivates a community of empowered individuals striving to make a positive impact.

The Power of Authentic Connections

The transformative potential of mentorship is fully realized when creating authentic connections. These connections are not merely transactional relationships but deeply personal bonds that encourage vulnerability, sharing, and mutual support. Examples like my aunt, who influenced me profoundly without even realizing it, show the lasting impact that authentic connections can have. These relationships inspire us to explore our potential, challenge our limitations, and embark on journeys of self-discovery and growth.

The presence of a mentor can be akin to a guiding light illuminating our path. Like a beacon of wisdom and encouragement, a mentor can inspire us. Within these genuine connections, we find solace in moments of uncertainty, courage in times of doubt, and resilience in the face of adversity.

Much like a gentle breeze that nudges a sapling to grow into a mighty oak, a mentor's influence can shape our beliefs, aspirations, and world perceptions. Their unwavering support is a sturdy foundation upon which we can build our dreams and aspirations, fostering a sense of empowerment and self-belief that propels us toward our goals.

Mentors and mentees are transformed profoundly. The mentor, through their guidance and wisdom, discovers new perspectives and insights, while the mentee, in turn, embarks on a journey of introspection and self-realization. Together, they create a symbiotic relationship that transcends mere acquaintance, blossoming into a profound bond that enriches their lives and empowers them to reach new heights.

Fostering Mutual Growth & Discovery

Modern mentorship is characterized by its reciprocal nature. It's a dynamic process where mentors and mentees learn from each other, challenge each other, and grow together. This mutuality ensures that mentorship is not a one-way street but a shared journey of discovery. It's about fostering an environment where everyone involved is a teacher and a learner, recognizing the value of diverse perspectives and experiences in driving personal and collective development.

In this collaborative approach to mentorship, mentors offer guidance, support, and wisdom based on their expertise and experience, while mentees bring fresh ideas, enthusiasm, and a willingness to learn. Through open communication, active listening, and mutual respect, both parties can create a supportive and empowering relationship that benefits them.

By embracing the idea that mentorship is a two-way street, individuals can maximize the potential for growth, inspiration, and success. This shared journey of discovery enriches the lives of those involved and contributes to a culture of continuous learning and development in all aspects of life.

Embracing the Mentorship Revolution

The mentorship revolution is not merely about transforming the mentor-mentee relationship but redefining how we approach personal and professional development in an interconnected world. By embracing modern mentorship principles—alignment, win-win situations, authenticity, and mutual growth—we can create meaningful, transformative experiences for ourselves and those we mentor.

As we navigate this journey, remember that the most profound lessons come from sharing our true selves and empowering others to do the same. Doing so fosters personal growth and fulfillment and contributes to a more authentic, empowered society.

This exploration of mentorship, inspired by my own experiences and the wisdom of those who have guided me, highlights the revolutionary potential of modern mentorship to inspire, transform, and enrich lives. As we embrace these principles, we step into a world where mentorship is not just about transferring knowledge but creating a legacy of growth, authenticity, and mutual success.

STEPH SHINABERY

About Steph Shinabery: Steph Shinabery is The World's Best Possibility Coach, and a Nurse Anesthesiologist, Artist, Speaker, and the Founder of GENIUS CODE ACADEMY.

After spending much of her life in a career that lacked the inspiration and fulfillment she knew was available to her, she began a journey to answer the question: "What is it I truly desire?"

Her journey led to the creation of the Genius Identity Code™, a process for unlocking your gift, purpose and path, and helping people see, believe and execute their unique genius to achieve miraculous outcomes.

Steph works with creative experts, entrepreneurs and coaches to help them embrace their authenticity and create a life that gets them excited to jump out of bed every day!

You can find her talk, "Wake Up Your Genius Machine" on Amazon Prime Video's *Speak Up: Empower Your Ideas, Season 4.*

Author's Website: *www.StephShinabery.com* & *www.GeniusCodeAcademy.com*

Book Series Website: *www.TheBookOfMentors.com*

TAYLOR L. COLE

DISCIPLE MAKING: WHO ARE YOU BECOMING

Today, there's a wealth of information and advice at our fingertips. From social media platforms to self-help books and various so-called authorities and experts, there's no shortage of people that are eager to share their knowledge, often at a cost. Everywhere we turn, influences from the world surround us, always ready to tempt and attract. Who do you trust to guide and mold your behaviors, habits and even your beliefs? How much do you allow the people and the environment around you to influence your decisions and choices?

It may surprise you, but you are knowingly or unknowingly being shaped by something or someone. Positive and negative influences, including role models, athletes, the news media, politicians, pro athletes, and celebrities are determining your next steps every day. Someone or something is teaching you how to live your life.

The only question is, did you choose it, or did it choose you? You have to consider who defines what is good and true and right in your life. Whose approval do you seek? Who shapes your beliefs? Who do you submit and surrender your preferences and expectations to? Who defines what success looks like? How do you navigate your next steps? A solid starting point is establishing a relationship with a reliable advisor who is continually expanding their knowledge while sharing it with others.

Discipleship and mentoring are closely connected. Both involve a process of guidance, teaching, and personal growth. Both discipleship and mentoring are intended to guide individuals from their current state to a new destination or level of growth. Both discipleship and mentoring encompass a transformative process with a student and a teacher, but discipleship goes beyond mere instruction. Simply put, a disciple is a student, learner, or follower who is becoming like the one they are following for the sake of others. A disciple is training and being trained to become like their teacher with a heart of generosity.

Christian discipleship is about intentionally investing in another person's spiritual growth, so they become more like Jesus. It is about stepping into the purpose and design that God intended for you as part of His perfect plan and taking someone along the journey with you. Jesus spent His life making disciples, so becoming like Jesus means that we too are called to mentor or make disciples.

If you haven't read *The Book of Mentors, Honoring Legacy Legend Zig Ziglar*, in that volume of the book series, I talk about how the Bible's Kingdom principles serve as a model for effective mentoring and discipleship. These Kingdom principles are displayed by Jesus in the growing relationship he shared with His students who later became teachers to countless others. Jesus is the best example of mentoring as demonstrated by the way He led and loved His disciples. Here are some of the principles.

- Selflessness (Philippians 2:3-8)
  - Jesus was truly focused on others and even gave up personal comforts to pursue His Father's mission. He was able to be submitted and under the authority of His Father.

  - He chose His followers who were each from different backgrounds, occupations, and ethnicities. He taught them to find unity amongst their differences.

  - He often provided free food for people, recognizing that people can rarely receive spiritual nourishment when they're in deep physical need.

  - He helped fishers catch fish.

- He healed the sick and never asked for anything in return. He even refused to take credit publicly.

- He voluntarily gave up His life so we could be forgiven of our sins, have eternal life and experience freedom today.

- He Paid it Forward (Matthew 4:18-20)
  - Jesus' disciples were challenged to "go and make disciples," meaning the mentor/mentee relationship didn't start and end with Jesus and the original disciples. He called them to pay it forward and mentor or disciple others.

- Truth is at His core (Luke 4:1-4)
  - Rather than relying on His own interpretations and conjecture, Jesus had an ultimate truth (God's word) that He stood on when He faced temptation and as He taught his disciples.

- Living by Example and Modeling the Behavior (John 13:14-17)
  - Jesus washed His disciples' feet. In that culture, washing feet was the lowest, nastiest job but Jesus did it to model serving in a radical way. While we probably won't feel led to wash our mentees' feet, we can radically lead by example and model a behavior that they'll want to emulate. Being humble and doing work that may not be the most lofty exemplifies the heart of a servant.

- Prayer (Matthew 6:9-13)
  - One day, the disciples came to Jesus and asked Him to teach them to pray. When we pray for our mentees or disciples, it keeps us focused on them and their needs, not just our own. Praying for their needs gives insight into their hearts. Praying for them is a way of actively loving them. Plus, we can pray for ourselves that we'll be good stewards of the gifts we've been entrusted with (which includes the students that follow us).

- Getting Started, Setting Boundaries, and Limits (John 2:1-11)
  - A good mentor will always be there for their mentee, but there's value in setting a specific beginning and ending date. It makes your time together more valuable, and it holds your student accountable

for making progress by a certain time. When we look at Jesus, we see He set boundaries and only mentored His disciples in the physical for about three years. This doesn't mean the friendship or the relationship ends, it means you're encouraging the student to prepare themselves to lead others and put what they've learned into practice.

These are the qualities to seek in the person you are emulating, so that you can extend generosity and, in turn, make disciples.

Dreaming of Your Future

Bob Proctor famously wrote, "All of the great achievers of the past have been visionary figures; they were men and women who projected into the future. They thought of what could be, rather than what already was, and then they moved themselves into action, to bring these things into fruition." As you consider your discipleship journey, do you have a vision for the future you? Is the person you are following projecting a better vision for your future than you can for yourself? Are they seeing potential in you that surpasses what you've imagined? Do they encourage and inspire you to dream?

My Daddy was one of the most creative people I've ever met. He had a knack for transforming everyday objects that he found at our ranch or around the house into artwork that the best galleries were eager to buy. He also had a special gift for seeing potential in people that they failed to see in themselves. Our cousin, Don, is an outstanding cook and would often hang around my dad, seek his advice, and observe the way he created things. Although Don never received formal training in culinary arts, his passion for cooking shined through deliciously in every dish.

Don had an idea to create a curly que potato dish for festivals and events but the potato cutters on the market couldn't withstand the high volume of use in his kitchen. It was frustrating for Don because he knew there had to be a better way, but he didn't know how to make it happen. My Daddy designed an automatic potato peeler that delicately sliced potatoes in half the time of commercial peelers, significantly reducing waste. On top of that, the potato peeler was also effective for pineapples and other fruits and vegetables, allowing Don to broaden his catering business.

Daddy helped him create a system so he could organize and store his products and even helped Don market his new business. My Daddy asked for nothing in return from Don except that he teach others what he learned. Don had a dream to share his passion for cooking and my dad had a big vision for who Don could become. The same characteristics for discipleship and becoming a disciple were part of the relationship: trust, selflessness, encouragement, modeling the behavior, and paying it forward.

Daddy believed in Don, cared about him, and wanted to pour into him. Don was teachable and willing to accept feedback. As discipleship mentors, one of the best things we get to do is inspire the mentee towards change. Most people are reluctant to change, but with the right leader beside them, they can change habits, lifestyles, and behaviors. The big questions the disciple or mentee has to ask themselves is, "Do I really want to change?" and "Do I believe that God can change me?"

Are you ready to change both as a disciple and one who is discipling others?

1. Ask someone you trust what it is that they see in you and invite them to come alongside you to help you get there.

2. Recognize that you'll have to decide to go a different way. Be willing to relinquish old habits, behaviors, beliefs, and even people, if they're not aligned with who you believe God is inviting you to become.

3. Pray for God to unveil His perfect plan for you and for your heart to be open and receptive to it.

4. Encourage someone by speaking life into their situation and assisting them in taking their next steps. Becoming a Christian disciple isn't purely for yourself, it's also in service to others.

TAYLOR L. COLE

About Taylor L. Cole: Taylor L. Cole is a seasoned professional dedicated to helping meaningful brands capture the attention they deserve. With a career spanning over 14 years, Taylor has honed her skills in Communications, PR, and social media, working with Fortune 500 companies, multi-national corporations, and startups across various industries including travel, tech, healthcare, and consumer products.

Starting her journey in the world of television while still in high school, Taylor quickly made her mark, producing her first major show as an undergraduate at Southern Methodist University. She has since taken on leadership roles in communications and public relations at renowned companies such as Kimberly Clark, Hotels.com, Expedia, and Sabre.

Taylor's extensive experience has allowed her to work with a diverse range of business owners, entertainers, and travel suppliers, teaching her the crucial lesson that brands must captivate their audience with the right marketing exposure to avoid falling into obscurity.

As a guide for brands and leaders, Taylor specializes in crafting effective messaging and on-camera strategies, featuring her clients on quality, international TV programs and podcasts. She is the executive producer and host of *The Focus* and *Speak Up* on Amazon Prime Video, as well as the travel TV show *Hotel Hunt*, where she explores stunning destinations and uncovers unique accommodations. Her latest project is *Workable Faith*, a show where she engages with business leaders about integrating faith into the marketplace.

Taylor is also a dedicated community member, serving on various non-profit boards, business leadership groups, and actively participating in her church. Her involvement includes roles with the American Diabetes

Association, Fellowship Power Lunch, Truth at Work, Valley Creek Church, and SMU.

In her free time, Taylor indulges her love for travel, rollercoasters, and warm buttery popcorn, all while helping leaders build and leave a lasting legacy. She invites brands ready to step into the spotlight to connect with her at TVwithTLC.com, where they can embark on a journey to refine their messaging, identify their key audience, and build the perfect platform to share their unique voice.

Taylor's specialties encompass a wide range of services including being a Brand Spokesperson, TV Host for Travel & Lifestyle Products, TV Production, Podcasting, Christian Businesses and Values-Based Initiatives, Author & Professional Speaker Visibility, Strategic Public Relations, Marketing Consulting, Communications Strategy, Media Coaching & Training, and serving as a Fractional Communications & PR Executive. She is the proven fixer that brands need to shine in their respective industries.

TLC

Author's Website: *www.TVWithTLC.com*

Book Series Website: *www.TheBookOfMentors.com*

VIKKI ROOD

THE GIFT OF GIVING BACK

In the garden of life, the most beautiful flowers bloom under the care of a dedicated gardener. I've had the privilege of nurturing many such blossoms, sharing the water and sunlight that was so generously given to me. This journey of mentoring is not just a path I chose; it chose me, wrapping its vines around my heart and teaching me the essence of giving, inspiring, and creating alongside those who are still finding their footing in this vast garden.

When I rewind to my childhood, I remember being eight years old, the elder sibling to twin brothers and a baby sister. Inevitably, I slipped into the role of a mentor. I was the one showing them the ropes—uncovering cool things, orchestrating games, eliciting laughter, and, often, playing the entertainer. This early experience sparked a lifelong fascination with people—understanding our motives, our actions, and how to create an environment where everyone feels valued and deserving of attention. The question that often danced in my mind was: How can we navigate life in a way that's both smooth and enjoyable?

Life, as we know, isn't always a straight path. It comes with its fair share of bumps, rainy days, and moments shrouded in fog. Through these times, I've discovered a powerful way to weather the storm—my chosen family. These are the people who truly know me, love me, and importantly, aren't afraid to tell me the truth. Whether it's a piece of food stuck in my teeth or if I'm being overly critical of myself, they're there to offer a reality check. They remind me of the power in choice—the ability to steer my life in a different direction when the current one isn't serving me.

Sharing What Was So Freely Given to Me

My journey into mentoring began on a day painted with the ordinary brush of routine. It wasn't marked by any particular sign or a dramatic turn of events. Instead, it was the realization that the wisdom, love, and support generously showered upon me by mentors of my own were gifts too precious to keep to myself. They were seeds meant to be sown into the lives of others, not treasures to be hoarded.

In every shared experience, every piece of advice given, and every moment of silence filled with understanding, I was passing on a legacy. This legacy was not built on monumental achievements or groundbreaking discoveries, but on simple acts of kindness, moments of vulnerability, and the courage to be genuinely oneself. It was about showing up, day after day, ready to give without the expectation of receiving.

Inspiring Others to Live in Their Authenticity

In the glossy pages of magazines and the curated perfection of social media feeds, it's easy to lose oneself in the pursuit of looking good. The world often feels like a race, where the finish line is adorned with the trappings of success and approval. Yet, in this relentless chase, the essence of who we are begins to blur.

As a mentor, one of my greatest missions is to inspire my mentees to embrace their authentic selves; to remind them that their worth is not tied to the applause of the crowd but resides in the quiet assurance of their uniqueness. Authenticity is the key that unlocks the doors to genuine happiness and fulfillment, and mentoring offers a platform to share this truth.

I've seen the transformative power of authenticity in action. It begins with a tentative step—a shared secret, a confessed dream, or a whispered fear. These moments of openness are like rays of sunlight breaking through the clouds, illuminating the path to self-discovery. By living authentically, I not only guide my mentees towards their own light but also reaffirm my commitment to my true self.

Allowing the Mentees Space to Make Decisions & Be Creative

True growth occurs in the spaces where we are free to explore, make mistakes, and find our own way. As a mentor, my role is not to dictate every step but to provide a safe and nurturing environment where creativity and decision-making flourish. It's about giving my mentees the room to spread their wings, knowing that the flight might be wobbly at first, but trusting in their ability to soar.

This approach requires letting go of control and embracing trust. It's about believing in the potential of my mentees, even when they struggle to see it themselves. Each decision they make, whether it leads to success or serves as a valuable lesson, is a step towards their independence and self-assurance.

The beauty of allowing creative freedom is in the unexpected outcomes. Creativity knows no bounds, and when mentees are empowered to think outside the box, they often surpass their own expectations. These moments of triumph are not just victories for the mentees but shared celebrations that reinforce the value of our interconnectedness.

The Interconnectedness that Matters

In a world that celebrates individualism, the concept of interconnectedness seems almost revolutionary. Yet, it is in our very nature to seek connection, to find solace in the presence of those who understand and share our journey. Mentoring, at its core, is an embodiment of this interconnectedness. It's a reminder that we are not islands, but part of a vast, intricate network of lives touching lives.

The mentor-mentee relationship is a beautiful illustration of this principle. It's a partnership that acknowledges the value of every individual's journey while recognizing that our paths are interwoven. We used to take care of each other in communities where every person's role was acknowledged, and through mentoring, we can recapture this sense of belonging and purpose.

This interconnectedness extends beyond the immediate relationships to influence the broader community. As mentees grow into their potential and start to share their own gifts, the ripple effect is profound. They become mentors in their own right, perpetuating the cycle of giving, inspiring, and creating. This chain reaction is a testament to the enduring power of our connections, proving that when we uplift one another, the entire community thrives.

Mentoring is more than just a role; it's a journey of mutual growth, discovery, and transformation. It's about sharing the wisdom that was so freely given to me, inspiring others to live authentically, and allowing them the space to discover for themselves what their truth is!

VIKKI ROOD

About Vikki Rood: Vikki Rood is a passionate advocate for joyful living, a seasoned empowerment coach, and a published author dedicated to helping individuals uncover their authentic selves and live lives filled with purpose, empowerment, and boundless joy. Vikki invites you to join her on a journey of self-discovery, empowerment, and joy.

Through coaching, workshops, and a thriving community, she'll help you uncover your authentic self, embrace your unique path, and find fulfillment in every facet of your life.

Author's Website: *www.VikkiRoodCoaching.com*

Book Series Website: *www.TheBookOfMentors.com*

WILLIAM BLAKE

ABSORB OR APPLY—WHICH IMPRESSES MENTORS?

"You want to be a magnet for what you want,
not a repellent for what you don't want."
~ **Bob Proctor**

You Don't Know Until You Try

It's wild how many times I've been so hyped about diving into something fresh, only to hit the brakes right after taking the plunge. Back when I was starting my self-development journey, two of my favorite mentors dropped a course on creating a mastermind to reach thousands. I was all in—I bought it, logged in, and absorbed every nugget of information they dished out. I had pages upon pages of notes from those videos. But then came the practical part. They talked about signing up for a Stripe account and doing Facebook marketing. One video in on that, I shut my laptop and didn't touch it for years.

What made me stop dead in my tracks? Fear. Plain and simple. I was scared of the unknown territory. I didn't have a clue about marketing on Facebook, and the idea of setting up a Stripe account felt like putting my sensitive information at risk. It was ironic—I loved soaking up all that information, but when it came to putting it into action, I froze and walked away.

Another instance that hit me hard was at a networking event. My good friend hosted these events regularly, and I figured since I wanted to be a speaker, I should start networking. Dressed to the nines, I got there half an hour early... and sat in my car until five minutes before kick-off. Walking in, I barely knew anyone except my friend. Feeling lost amidst a sea of business pros, I headed to a corner table, hoping to blend in. Then came the mastermind part where we shared our business stories in groups. I felt utterly out of place, surrounded by folks I couldn't relate to. By the end, I was totally deflated.

Looking back at these moments, one thing rang clear: I loved absorbing information. But when it boiled down to applying it, I chickened out. Thankfully, I've outgrown that habit of inaction, but the fear of new things still lingers. That's where the real growth happens, though.

Fast forward five years, I kickstarted my coaching business. I knew I had to tackle things I had zero clue about and do it fast. Following another mentor's advice, I committed to having 500 conversations in a week. Boy, did I bite off more than I could chew! The first 100 were a struggle, the next 100 a tad easier, but the last 300? That's where it hit me—I hadn't factored in the need to keep conversations rolling! It wasn't just reaching out; it was about sustaining those connections. But you know what? Amidst the challenge, I had some amazing chats, landed great calls, and even gained paying clients.

You only discover what you don't know by actually doing something you've never done before.

Network Like Someone's Watching... Because They Are

Over the last decade, I've learned the value of building a solid professional network and seizing opportunities. How can you achieve that? By diving headfirst into unfamiliar and mundane tasks day in, day out.

If you're aiming for a strong professional network and opportunities, it boils down to two things. Firstly, get out there. It's baffling when folks complain about lacking connections and opportunities while spending their days wasting time. One example could be gaming. Don't get me wrong—I love gaming and make time for it weekly. But if you're not out there engaging with people, how do you expect to build those connections? There's a mismatch between logic and personal action. Logic screams that more exposure means more people met, but our emotions or conditioning cloud that truth.

Secondly, the more you do, the more you receive. It's as simple as that. Remember the book, *The Go-Giver* by Bob Burg? The last law's about receiving. Give and you shall receive. By being visible, meeting more people, and diving into opportunities, you attract high-level connections. You find them by being where they are.

Like I said, I like gaming, but high-performing pros aren't hanging out there all the time. So, I make time for networking, attend mastermind groups, show up at friends' events, add value on social media—all knowing that the more I put out, the more comes back. The opportunities and connections you seek will come your way when you go after them.

Now, let's dive into practical networking strategies that have been game-changers in my journey and can hopefully help in yours. Networking isn't just about attending events; it's about strategic engagement. One highly effective strategy I found is leveraging online platforms. Platforms like LinkedIn, Facebook, and even industry-specific forums offer a goldmine of opportunities to connect with professionals.

Start by optimizing your profiles with relevant information, engaging content, and a professional yet approachable tone. Don't hesitate to join groups or discussions within your niche. Engaging thoughtfully in conversations and sharing valuable insights can organically attract like-minded individuals and potential mentors to your network.

Additionally, don't underestimate the power of in-person events and meetups. While online connections are invaluable, face-to-face interactions can foster deeper relationships. When attending events, set specific goals—whether it's meeting three new people or initiating conversations with industry leaders.

Approach networking with authenticity and curiosity. Ask open-ended questions, actively listen, and offer help or insights where you can. Remember, networking isn't just about what you can gain; it's about building mutually beneficial relationships.

The Reciprocal Mentorship

Mentorship's more like a two-way street than a lecture hall. Take my connection with a mentor I'll call John, for instance.

Our story kicked off in a local coffee house, a mutual friend get-together that turned into a game-changer. Little did I know that this encounter would set the stage for a mentorship that was about more than just taking notes from a sage. Initially, John's openness and willingness to share his ideas struck a chord with me. It wasn't until later that I discovered he was impressed by what he saw in me—call it a spark or a drive—that resonated with him. That initial vibe ignited the beginning of our mentor-mentee connection.

What began as attending John's events quickly morphed into something deeper. I didn't just hang around; I jumped in, lending a hand wherever I could. Eventually, I took the plunge, ditching my job to team up with John directly, learning the tricks of the trade. But here's the kicker—this mentorship wasn't just about what John gave me; it was about what I brought to the table.

As time passed, our relationship matured into a partnership rooted in mutual value. It wasn't the typical mentor-mentee scene; it was more like a back-and-forth exchange—sharing insights, solving problems, and genuinely supporting each other. It wasn't solely about learning from John; it was about being a part of his journey, offering solutions, and diving into challenges together. It was this give-and-take that transformed our dynamic from mentor and mentee to trusted pals and collaborators.

That's the key—more than just seeking advice in a single meetup. It's about embodying the essence of what you aspire to become and allowing them to witness that within you. First impressions matter, but the real depth comes from demonstrating your commitment. Attending their events, offering assistance, providing genuine value—those actions transform a fleeting encounter into a relationship of mutual exchange. It's not merely about transactions; it's about fostering a reciprocal connection.

Seeking a mentor goes beyond mere desire—it's about living the essence of what you aim to achieve. Your mentor won't magically appear unless you mirror the path you aspire to walk. Staying on your course without embodying the traits you seek makes it challenging to find that guiding figure. Actively immerse yourself in spaces where potential mentors thrive and watch as opportunities unfold. Opening yourself to more opportunities means encountering new faces and potential mentors, igniting an upward trajectory toward growth.

Here's the crux of it all—take that leap, immerse yourself in the mentorship mindset, and witness the magic unfold. Challenge yourself to step into the realm of action, embracing every opportunity to learn, act, and iterate. It's in this cycle that growth thrives. So, get out there, infuse yourself with the mentor vibe, and watch as mentors and opportunities gravitate towards your relentless pursuit. This is your journey—seize it, shape it, and make every moment count!

WILLIAM BLAKE

About William Blake: William is a speaker and motivator. He focuses on the skill sets of learning, listening, and observing to help people access new avenues of success and solutions. What might seem like regular everyday skills that most overlook, William teaches people how to find creative ways of accessing those skills.

William Blake is a stalwart professional in the world of organization, strategy, and methods. Being diagnosed with Dyslexia at a young age and struggling with reading and speaking, William is an example that through perseverance, any challenge can become a superpower.

William spearheads a dynamic coaching and speaking venture, empowering dyslexics to harness their unique strengths and embrace a world of boundless possibilities. He is also one of the chapter team leaders and corporate associates at Champion Circle Networking Association founded by Speaker Jon Kovach Jr.

From speaking to youth to being a camp counselor at Idaho Diabetes Youth Programs, William loves volunteering and helping children and teens believe in themselves and their unlimited potential. And of most importance to William is his love for his family. With his wife, he is dedicated to raising his daughters in a world of greatness, happiness, and unlimited belief.

Author's website: *www.WilliamBlakeLight.com*

Book Series Website: *www.TheBookOfMentors.com*

"THE POWER OF YOUR THOUGHTS DETERMINES THE QUALITY OF YOUR LIFE."

~ BOB PROCTOR

Habitude Warrior Mastermind

Join a team of
AWESOME
Entrepreneurs, Coaches, Business Owners, and Leaders to support you in your journey of success!

Be one of my personal guests for a session!
www.MastermindGuestPass.com

HABITUDE WARRIOR & INTEGRITY PUBLISHING EDITORIAL TEAM

Habitude Warrior International and Integrity Publishing take great pride in our editorial team who put their sweat, tears, and heart into each and every project and national bestseller! Thank you team!

JON KOVACH JR.
Team Manager

Jon Kovach Jr. strives to assist every author and every team member in the process of self-development for ultimate success.

PAT MINTON
VP of Operations

Pat Minton has been with the Habitude Warrior International team for over 20 years getting her start with Brian Tracy & Erik Swanson.

JILLIAN KOVACH
Editorial Manager

Jillian is a vital team member of Habitude Warrior & Integrity Publishing bringing her expertise managing our Editorial Department.

FATIMA HURD
Editorial Team & Photographer

Fatima is our Professional Photographer for Habitude Warrior as well as one of our members on the Proofing Department team.

LAUREN COBB
Editorial Team Member

Lauren Cobb is part of our Proofing Department for Habitude Warrior & Integrity Publishing as well as one of our authors.

To inquire about joining our team please send us an email to Team@HabitudeWarrior.com